Start Your Own

COLLEGE PLANNING CONSULTANT BUSINESS

Additional titles in *Entrepreneur's* Startup Series

Start Your Own

Entrepreneur
MAGAZINE'S

start*up*

Start Your Own

COLLEGE PLANNING CONSULTANT BUSINESS

*Your Step-by-Step
Guide to Success*

Entrepreneur Press and Eileen Figure Sandlin

EP
Entrepreneur
PRESS®

Entrepreneur Press, Publisher
Cover Design: Beth Hansen-Winter
Production and Composition: Eliot House Productions

This publication is designed to provide accurate and authoritative information in regard to
the subject matter covered. It is sold with the understanding that the publisher is not engaged
in rendering legal, accounting or other professional services. If legal advice or other expert
assistance is required, the services of a competent professional person should be sought.

ebook ISBN: 978-1-61308-246-1

Contents

Preface

There's an old saying that nothing is certain but taxes and death. Whoever came up with that gloomy expression (allegedly the illustrious Benjamin Franklin) obviously didn't have to worry about putting kids through college, or that might have been on the short list, too.

According to the Institute of Education Sciences, a federal entity dedicated to collecting data related to education in the United States, a record 21.6 million students attended American colleges and universities in the fall of 2012, nearly a 29 percent increase since fall 2000. Of those students, the U.S. Census Bureau says, more than 4.4 million were in the 15–19 age bracket, the market primed and ready for the advice dispensed by college consultants. And the really excellent news is, every fall a new crop of college-students-to-be enters high school and looks forward to a stint at one of America's 4,495 degree-granting educational institutions.

That's where you come in. Using counseling skills you may have already honed in a secondary education setting, or knowledge you've gained from other relevant sources, you can make a difference in the lives of these eager young scholars, while building a viable and satisfying business for yourself.

This book covers all the intel you need to establish and launch a successful college consulting business. Among the topics it covers are:

- Statistics relevant to the academic community
- Tips for establishing a home office
- Market research to help you reach your target audience
- Business professionals who can help you do business better
- Naming the business
- Professional resources
- Cyber techniques (including websites and social media)
- Advertising and public relations tactics
- Financial strategies
- And much more

Within these pages you'll also find worksheets related to the business startup process that you can use to brainstorm, estimate your own expenses, and track income and expenses.

What this book *doesn't* cover, however, are the skills and techniques used in the actual consulting process. It's assumed you already have or will develop those skills on your own, or will learn them from respected organizations like the Independent Educational Consultants Association (IECA). Instead, we invite you to use this book as a roadmap on the way to establishing a professional and efficient homebased business that allows you to use your expert consulting skills to develop and improve tomorrow's leaders.

Class is now in session. Please turn the page and settle in.

1

Your Higher Calling

Busy lifestyles have spawned them. Nearly 4,500 institutions of higher learning have made them possible. More than 21 million students have created a demand for them. And now you can take advantage of today's ever-growing need for college admissions consulting services by throwing your hat—or shall we say mortarboard?—into this interesting and rewarding arena.

Today's college planning consultants—a term used interchangeably in this book with educational consultants or college admissions/financial aid consulting professionals—offer a wide array of valuable services to students and their parents. For instance, they help steer high school students to the academic, extracurricular, and athletic pursuits that will increase their chances of being admitted to the college(s) of their choice. They help students wade through the mounds of paperwork necessary to apply for both college admission and financial aid, and they make sure the forms are submitted on time. They also specialize in helping at-risk students, learning-disabled students, and other nontraditional students achieve their highest potential. In extreme cases, they may even help save lives, which may sound dramatic until you consider that placing at-risk young people firmly on the path to college success truly can help them avoid making bad lifestyle choices that could negatively impact the rest of their lives.

Head of the Class

According to the Independent Educational Consultants Association (IECA), some of the best and most capable educational consultants come from the ranks of the country's experienced academic advisors and counselors, who gain hands-on experience at both public and private universities, colleges, and secondary and elementary schools. (Or at any rate, they have the easiest time making the transition to educational consulting, given their background, says Mark Sklarow, executive director of IECA. See "Background Check" on page 3 for more information.) In addition, they often have titles like certified educational planner (CEP) or licensed educational psychologist, as well as an alphabet soup of other prestigious academic letters after their names, including Ph.D., MBA, M.A., Ed.D. (Doctor of Education), and Ed.M. (Master of Education). On the financial aid side, some consultants are even CPAs or credentialed financial planners.

Both this experience and educational background are important for someone who wishes to hang out a shingle as an educational consultant, because frankly, the college admissions field in general and the financial aid consulting industry in particular both have a rather unsavory reputation. The popular press frequently warns the public

Fun Fact

The SAT was introduced in 1926 to measure the academic achievements of students bound for college. Although the name has undergone numerous changes over the years (the acronym once stood for Scholastic Aptitude Test), the College Board says the initials don't stand for anything anymore. However, *The Princeton Review* irreverently says SAT stands for "Stupid, Annoying Test."

Background Check

There's a prevailing notion that private school, high school, and college counselors make the best educational consultants because they have spent so much time with kids, have read students' files, are familiar with standardized tests, and so on. But according to Mark Sklarow, executive director of the Independent Educational Consultants Association (IECA), a counseling background isn't mandatory to be successful in this field.

"In my experience, counselors have the easiest time making the transition [from education to educational consulting]," he says. "They definitely get the one-on-one stuff. But although they understand the administrative part of counseling, they usually lack small-business skills. Also, they usually only know their own school or college and the surrounding area but usually not much beyond that. In addition, they usually don't see the learning-disabled kids or the ones who don't know what they want out of life. So they have a steep learning curve just like someone who doesn't come from academic counseling."

Conversely, Sklarow says that some of the other people who come to IECA, including everyone from lawyers to real estate agents, understand the small-business picture but lack the hands-on academic piece of the consulting pie. So what's an aspiring educational consultant to do? To begin with, look for a mentor who will allow you to work with him or her to learn the ropes. Then join an organization like IECA, the Higher Education Consultants Association, or the National Association for College Admission Counseling. You'll find more information about these groups in Chapter 7.

about shady consultants who gleefully scam unsuspecting families of limited means who are desperate to find the best college and/or aid package. They report that consultants charge ridiculous fees, up to and including an exorbitant percentage of the financial aid package. They've also written about how some unscrupulous consultants "guarantee" that they can get a child a full ride at a competitive university, then slink away, retainer fee in hand, leaving the student and his or her parents high and dry.

Then there are the dabblers, or the people whom Santa Fe, New Mexico, educational consultant Whitney Laughlin, Ed.D., refers to as the "Mommy Corps." These are the aspiring consultants who come by their knowledge of the college application process from having shepherded an offspring or two through the experience, and may even have succeeded in getting said children admitted to a prominent university. They figure that having navigated the choppy waters of college admission successfully, they have the right stuff to turn their knowledge into a thriving career. In some cases, they have degrees themselves, although more often than not, those degrees are in fields other than education or counseling.

But what the dabblers usually don't have is insider knowledge of a wide variety of college campuses the way professional counselors do. They don't know the right people at the university level to contact for insight and information. They also don't have experience dealing with complex personalities and figuring out how to match kids to the institution where they'll thrive and grow. In short, they're trying to build a business without paying their dues—and that can be a real handicap when it comes to running a successful educational consultancy.

"The college admissions process may seem intuitive, but it's based on a cumulative process of experience that includes visiting colleges; going to conferences, seminars, and workshops; and knowing enough about various colleges to help students pick the right one," Sklarow says. "The person who says, 'I got my daughter into Bryn Mawr, and it was so much fun that I can't wait to help others get into college, too,' won't have enough knowledge to connect the right kid to the right college. You have to go out and visit 40 or 60 colleges, so when you meet a kid, you have an *aha* moment and recognize that he seems like a Penn State kid, for example, rather than a Temple kid."

Stat Fact

There are approximately 24,651 public high schools in the United States. The top three schools in 2012, according to *Newsweek's* "100 Best High Schools in America" list, were School for the Talented and Gifted, Dallas, Texas; Thomas Jefferson High School for Science and Technology, Alexandria, Virginia; and School of Science and Engineering Magnet, Dallas, Texas.

Getting an Education

Don't get us wrong. Our point here isn't to discourage you from pursuing a career in educational consulting if you don't have decades of academic counseling experience. It *is* possible to build a career in this field if you have the drive and determination, a willingness to invest time on professional development, and a commitment to excellence. But there's no question that people with previous admissions experience have an edge, and that it will take a lot of work to develop the knowledge and contacts you'll need to do the job right if you don't have that experience. And as Sklarow points out, you'll also have to travel extensively to visit college campuses and get to know what they offer, and it usually will be at your own expense. Universities generally pay expenses only for experienced consultants because they're the ones who are most likely to make successful placements at their institutions.

Whether you're a relative neophyte or an experienced counselor, this book will provide you with the tools and insight you'll need to launch a college admissions and financial aid consulting business. In the chapters ahead, we'll cover all the business basics, from establishing your company as a legal entity to outfitting a home office, handling the finances, promoting your services, and so on. We'll assume you already have the basic knowledge you need to help young students realize their dream of attending the university of their choice. If you do need assistance with how to counsel eager young students, make college placements, advise about financial aid packages, or otherwise run the educational consulting side of the business, you'll find it helpful to join an organization like IECA. You can also check out the professional development opportunities discussed at length in Chapter 7.

Class Picture

In the meantime, before we delve into the nuts and bolts of running your own homebased, college-planning business, a little background on this industry is helpful.

IECA estimates that in the United States, there are only about 4,000–5,000 educational consultants, just over 700 of whom belong to its organization. This is strictly a guess, because not everyone who provides educational consulting services chooses to join a professional membership association like IECA. (In fact, IECA estimates there are another 10,000–15,000 "dabblers.") But using a figure of 5,000 as a benchmark, that works out to about one consultant per 3,400 students (based on a student population of more than 21 million). What's more, IECA says that some states—including Idaho and Oklahoma—do not yet have even a single educational consultant within their borders.

Even the federal government doesn't track educational consultants as a specialized group. The closest thing to a classification for this group of professionals can be found in the *2012–2013 Occupational Outlook Handbook* (U.S. Department of Labor). The handbook has a "School and Career Counselors" category, which includes school counselors who work in public and private schools. But no information is included there about college counselors in particular. A second counselor category, "Educational, Guidance, School, and Vocational Counselors," could be where the independent college counselors lurk, but no one really knows for sure!

What is known is that with that pool of more than 21 million college-minded students mentioned earlier, the opportunities for an enterprising consultant like you to forge a meaningful career doing something you love appear very bright indeed.

History 101

Just as statistics on who's who in educational consulting are as scarce as undergrads in the library during spring break, so is historical data about the profession. As might be expected, we know far more about the genesis of education in America than we know about the practice of admissions consulting. The first institution of higher learning in the United States actually predates the Union by nearly a century and a half. Harvard College, which is the oldest school of Harvard University, was founded in 1636, a mere 16 years after the Pilgrims landed at Plymouth Rock, and opened its doors to just nine students. Seven years later, the first scholarship in history was awarded at Harvard thanks to the largess of a private donor, Lady Anne Radcliffe Mowlson.

Fast-forward to the 20th century. It's believed that educational consultants have been around in one form or another for decades, but it wasn't until the 1950s, with the advent of SAT test-preparation classes, that the career truly began to gain momentum, mostly because parents started realizing that there was a way they could give their kids an edge. One of the earliest consulting programs—if not the earliest—was established in 1968 by Howard Greene, M.A., M.Ed., who still consults with schools and colleges today. Sklarow of IECA says that the *nouveau riche* fueled that early demand for educational consultants because they were interested in sending their offspring to boarding school but didn't know where to turn for insider information. As a result, members-only golf clubs and other places where the privileged gathered became the arenas where information about how to get into the most elite schools—or who could help—was exchanged.

It wasn't long before those who offered boarding school admissions advice realized that offering college admissions counseling could be far more lucrative. After all, there were about 3,000 students in private boarding schools at the time vs. 1 million college students. So while the shift from consulting for boarding schools to colleges developed slowly, Sklarow's theory is that the field really took off when educational

Fun Fact

The first public high school in the United States (now called English High School) was founded in Boston in the winter of 1821 and was open to any boy aged 12 or older who could pass the entrance exam. This was a revolutionary idea for its time, because advanced learning previously had been open only to the wealthy.

consultants stopped apologizing about their livelihood and started focusing on educating parents and students on how they could help them get into the college best suited to their talents and academic abilities.

Sklarow says, "We'd see people stand up at conferences and meetings and say, 'I'm an educational consultant—I know, I'm sorry about that.' But the fact is, 'our' kids are more likely to graduate and to go to private universities. As a result there's been a fundamental shift in attitude about the profession, and in particular, our impact has been dramatic at small liberal arts colleges. An awful lot of kids [who go there] have worked with IECA members."

> **Smart Tip** Tip...
>
> When visiting college campuses, be sure to bring along a camera and journal in which you can note your impressions about the campus as well as details about the academic and social environment, athletics, housing, and other characteristics. Once you've visited several colleges, they all start to look alike, so having notes will be very helpful later.

Today, those kids' parents are no longer just the wealthy and privileged. Overwhelmingly, they're suburban professionals who want to make sure they find the best possible educational environment and financial assistance for their budding scholars. And Sklarow says there's yet another market percolating right now. "The middle class in both urban and suburban areas have more of a need to know about financial aid than ever," he says. "That means there will be a greater need for consultants to help them."

Steven Antonoff, an educational consultant in Denver, says another trend today is consultants helping clients choose schools. "There is a great demand for consultants who know the process to get Junior through the college application experience, but it's important to be knowledgeable about college environments and how Junior will fit in," he says. "Good consultants are both process- and knowledge-oriented."

Who Needs You?

You'll find most of your clientele are likely to come from the following demographics:

- Busy parents who have neither the time nor the energy to do all the legwork necessary to find the right college for their kids.
- Parents who value time more than money and would rather spend what free time they have on personal and/or family pursuits and pay someone to pore over college catalogs or applications for them.
- Parents who want or need their kids to have more personal attention than is usually available from high school counselors. "School counselors are so

overworked," Sklarow says. "Today's counselors have an average of 600 kids to counsel, or up to 1,000 or more in schools in large cities like Los Angeles. They're often dealing with drugs and alcohol, crisis intervention, and even lunchroom duty, so college counseling usually is a really low priority."

- Parents who know other people who use educational consultants and feel their kid(s) will be at a disadvantage if they don't use a consultant.

- People who are overwhelmed by or impatient with the application process (so much paperwork, so little time!). This is especially true when it comes to financial aid, which of course must be reapplied for every year.

- Parents who are anxiety-ridden about getting their kids into the "best" schools. "It used to be simple: If a kid's SAT scores were good, she would go to Penn," says Sklarow. "If the SAT scores were lower, that same kid would go to Temple. Now, almost the entire senior year is given over to college anxiety."

America's Top Colleges

- ○ Harvard University
- ○ Princeton University
- ○ Yale University
- ○ Columbia University
- ○ University of Chicago
- ○ Massachusetts Institute of Technology
- ○ Stanford University
- ○ Duke University
- ○ University of Pennsylvania
- ○ California Institute of Technology
- ○ Dartmouth College
- ○ Northwestern University
- ○ Johns Hopkins University
- ○ Washington University in St. Louis
- ○ Brown University
- ○ Cornell University
- ○ Rice University
- ○ University of Notre Dame
- ○ Vanderbilt University
- ○ Emory University
- ○ Georgetown University
- ○ University of California Berkeley
- ○ Carnegie Mellon University
- ○ University of California Los Angeles

Source: *U.S. News & World Report,* "Best Colleges 2013"

- People who perceive educational consultants as insiders (which of course you will be once you establish the right contacts) and as a result are in the best position to help them make the wisest collegial decisions.

So how can you serve these diverse audiences well? To begin with, you'll need to make the college circuit in person to glean as much insight as possible about local universities, Ivy League schools, Big 10 schools, and other nationally known schools, or all of these, depending on your personal interests and your clients' choices. Because there are nearly 4,500 colleges and universities in the United States and only one you, you may wish to follow the lead of educational consultants who choose to specialize in particular fields or offer specialized services. For instance, there are counselors who focus on Ivy League placements, others who counsel learning-disabled (LD) or at-risk kids, and still others who place athletes or performing arts students. Also, you'll need to get some education yourself, both as a business owner and as a student of educational consulting. You'll find insight on both in subsequent chapters of this book.

On the Money

You're no doubt wondering whether the financial rewards of being an educational consultant are worth the significant efforts necessary to establish your business, considering all the traveling, fact-finding, student meetings, office administration, and other tasks you'll be doing. The short answer is: Yes, eventually. Like most business startups, there's a learning curve and a corresponding earnings lag. That's why the entrepreneurs we spoke to for this book say that if you're contemplating establishing a college admissions and financial aid consulting business, you might want to make it a sideline rather than full-time pursuit in the beginning.

"We typically tell new consultants that they are likely to have a net loss in the first year because of the learning, traveling, campus tours, and office equipment they'll need," Sklarow says. "They can expect to break even or earn up to $15,000 in the second year, then be making a real salary in the third. The caution is: It all depends upon how effective you are in the marketing and promotion of your business."

Smart Tip

Tip...

A useful reference book you should have on your desk is *The Best 377 Colleges* (Princeton Review). It's a compilation of comments from 122,000 college students on everything from college classes to social activities, and includes information about admissions and financial aid. It's updated annually so the 411 is always fresh.

▲

"Since you won't make money right away, you should keep your day job," adds Steven Antonoff. "The sole exception is if you happen to be someone who doesn't need an immediate income or you're not income-dependent because there's a second breadwinner in your family."

Here's the scoop from IECA on how much you can earn once you get that academic ball rolling.

The average rate charged by educational consultants is about $140 an hour, with a range of about $75 to $300. Sklarow says about a third of consultants charge by the hour. The national average package cost for a college placement (typically starting in 10th or 11th grade through college enrollment) is $3,600, with a range of $750 to $6,000. There are exceptions to this rule, of course—we've heard of one consultant who charges (and gets) $42,000 for unlimited consulting time beginning in the eighth grade. But that's an extreme example. Most consultants cater to middle-class families, and as such, charge less to attract them.

So let's do some math. If you have 10 paying customers who choose your $3,600 package, your gross annual income would be $36,000. Or if you counseled 25 kids a year—which is entirely feasible by your third year—you would earn $90,000 a year.

Conversely, if you counsel 10 hours a week at $150 an hour, your annual income for a 45-week year would be $67,500 (the other seven weeks would be set aside for vacation and travel to campuses). So as you can tell, there is some serious money to be made once your business is up and running. The trick is to survive those lean and hungry early years.

Voices of Experience

In the chapters that follow, you'll learn everything you need to know to launch your new college admissions and financial aid consulting business. But perhaps what may

Fun Fact
There are 850 colleges and universities in the United States that make admission decisions without considering SAT or ACT scores. Although the list *doesn't* include the highest ranked institutions, selective schools like American University, Arizona State University, California State Polytechnic University, Sarah Lawrence college, and Texas A&M are all test-optional.

prove in the long run to be even more valuable to you is the input and views of the experienced educational consultants who agreed to be interviewed for this book. You'll find their insight and comments interspersed throughout the book. In addition, these entrepreneurs have agreed to serve as a resource for you if you ever have general questions pertaining to your new career. These entrepreneurs include:

- *Steven R. Antonoff, Ph.D., CEP, Antonoff Associates, Denver*: This published author has been an educational consultant since 1981 and has worked with more than 3,500 students. One of his books, *College Match: A Blueprint for Choosing the Best School for You* (Octameron Associates), will be of particular interest to aspiring educational consultants like you, because it focuses on how to make good decisions when matching students to universities. Previously he served as dean of students, then as dean of admission and financial aid, at the University of Denver, where he also earned his Ph.D. in psychology and human communications studies. He also holds an M.A. degree in education from the University of Denver and a B.S. in psychology from the University of Colorado. In addition to consulting, Antonoff has served as IECA's dean of education and training programs, teaches online college consulting courses through the UCLA Extension certificate program, and does a lot of public speaking.

- *Joan Bress, LCSW, CEP, College Resource Associates, Worcester, Massachusetts*: Bress has more than 25 years' experience as an educator and licensed clinical social worker (LCSW), with a specialty in adolescent development and family therapy. Since establishing her consulting practice in 1999, she has worked with students with many interests, although performing arts is an area of particular interest to her. She is an oft-published writer of articles on college issues for both local and national publications, and she often presents college prep seminars and workshops for students, parents, and teachers. She holds a master of social work (MSW) degree from Simmons College School of Social Work in Boston, an M.A. in romance languages from Boston University, and a B.A. degree in Spanish literature from the University of Pennsylvania.

- *James C. Heryer, M.A., CEP, College Guidance and Placement, Kansas City, Missouri*: This certified educational planner has been a college consultant since 1989. Formerly he was director of college placement at the Pembroke Hill School, Kansas City, and as a result has long-standing associations with numerous college admissions personnel. He has a bachelor's degree in business administration and economics from the University of Redlands in California and a master's degree in history from the University of Missouri Kansas City.

- *Charlotte Klaar, Ph.D., CEP, College Consulting Services, Brunswick, Maryland*: A self-employed educational consultant since 1995, Klaar holds a B.A. degree from Excelsior College, a master's in interdisciplinary science studies from

Johns Hopkins University, and a Ph.D. in general psychology from Capella University. She also holds a teaching certificate on the graduate level from the same institution. She has three educational consulting offices, one in Maryland, one in Massachusetts, and another in Virginia, and is a past adjunct instructor in the UCLA Extension certificate program in college counseling. She also has taught in the IECA Summer Training Institute for more than a decade.

- *Whitney Laughlin, Ed.D., Whitney Laughlin Ed.D. Educational Consultant, Victoria, British Columbia, and Santa Fe, New Mexico*: Laughlin began her educational career in 1971 as an ESL and Spanish teacher in a Mayan village in Yucatan, Mexico. Since then, she has had an eclectic career in education, ranging from director of admissions and financial aid to college counselor. She also is the director and founder of College Horizons Program, a summer pregraduate school program for Native American college students. She earned an Ed.D. degree in educational administration and nonprofit management from the University of California at Berkeley, an Ed.M. degree in administration, planning, and social policy from Harvard Graduate School of Education, and an M.A. in Spanish and women's studies from Goddard College in Plainfield, Vermont. Over the course of her 25 years in education, she has visited more than 500 college campuses. She founded her consulting business in 1996.

- *W. Judge Mason, M.A., Judge Mason Educational Consultant, Sedona, Arizona*: An educational consultant since 2001, Mason holds a bachelor's degree in philosophy from Yale and master's degrees in East Asian studies from Harvard and in English from Wayne State University in Detroit. He has decades of educational experience, ranging from teaching at International Christian University in Japan to serving as dean of students, academic dean and college counselor at various educational institutions. He is a founding member of the Southwest Boarding Schools and Western Boarding Schools, and a former member of the governing board of IECA.

- *Sarah Soule, Sarah Soule & Associates, Burlington, Vermont*: Soule has more than 20 years' experience working with college applicants, early in her career as the coordinator of group travels for the Northern Vermont Consortium of Colleges (for which she also served as president) and now as director of admissions and college counseling at Vermont Commons School in South Burlington, Vermont. She was named Admissions Counselor of the Year in 1997 by the New England Association of College Admissions Counselors and founded her part-time consulting business in 2003. She is a graduate of Johnson State College in Johnson, Vermont, with a B.A. in English, and holds a certification in elementary education.

College Catalog

If you're a college graduate (and maybe several times over), think back for a moment to your first day on campus. Do you remember being thrilled and exhilarated at the very adult venture upon which you were about to embark, yet somewhat intimidated and possibly even a little scared at the same time? And if this first-day experience took place on a campus far from home, you probably felt disoriented and somewhat lost, as well.

That first-day experience is probably universal for all college kids, even the jocks who would never admit it as they swagger in on all-expenses-paid sports scholarships. And as if that uncertainty isn't enough, research shows that many of these students will find that the college they have selected isn't the best match for their skills and talents. In fact, one study indicated that only 25 percent of kids earn degrees at the college they enter as a freshman. The universal experience for the other 75 percent is that they must expend a lot of money, time and energy starting all over and searching for the right educational environment, after having wasted big bucks and irretrievable time on courses that may not transfer to their new college.

Your task as an educational consultant will be to steer that 75 percent (or as many as you can get your hands on) to the best college for them right from the start. But of course, before you can start doing that noble and satisfying work, you need to establish a viable business and complete the due diligence necessary to hone your own skills and abilities. In the chapters that follow, you'll find advice about how to set up your business, how to promote it, and how to make the financials work. In the meantime, however, here's a look at the various services offered by educational consultants and the day-to-day operations necessary to run this type of business.

Course Offerings

The college-planning services typically offered by an educational consultant include:

- *College search/selection advice.* Matching a student to the college where he or she will fit in best and thrive is probably the consultant's most important job. Your insider knowledge about the student body, faculty, and atmosphere of various educational institutions, which you'll glean from campus visits, will help you steer students toward the institution where they'll be most successful.

- *Admissions process insight.* Consultants share their behind-the-scenes

> **Tip...**
>
> **Smart Tip**
> Success in this industry isn't just about the money. Rather, it's about having a genuine interest in kids, being excited about their dreams and goals, and cheering them on to succeed at the college to which you've matched them. The financial rewards can be great, but the personal satisfaction will make you richer every time.

knowledge of what it takes to be admitted to the most competitive colleges to give students the best chance of getting in.

- *Application assistance.* Consultants often help students fill in the blanks, then follow up with their student charges to make sure the applications are filed in time and with the correct application fee.

- *Admission essay assistance.* Consultants won't write an essay for a student, but they will look it over and offer advice on what information should go into it and how to make it more effective.

- *College visit assistance.* Consultants in the know can keep parents informed about college open houses and give advice on how to make the most of their college visits.

- *Evaluation of high school activities.* By reviewing a high school student's transcripts, test scores, extracurricular activities, and other accomplishments, a consultant can advise a student on the right moves to make while still in high school, from taking rigorous college prep courses to participating in particular activities or being tutored to improve grades. Being able to show a history of excellence in various activities can make a college admissions officer take notice, thus improving a student's chances of being admitted.

High Finance

When it comes to financial aid services, many educational consultants prefer to leave the financial aid consulting to people like accountants and certified financial planners. But it's not uncommon for them to offer advice and instruction on the basics of financial aid as a professional courtesy. For instance, they might give parents insight into how to pay for college or may direct them to scholarship resources. (Some educational consultants work with a financial planner and direct all questions about financial aid to that person when the need arises.) They also may help them fill out scholarship applications, which is a valued service for data-challenged people who don't have much time to spare or the patience necessary to work with the often-confusing forms. Just log on to www.fafsa.ed.gov and take a look at the Free Application for Federal Student Aid (FAFSA), the government form most colleges require from financial aid applicants, and you'll instantly know what we mean.

What consultants don't do, however, is guarantee that a certain amount of financial aid will be awarded, or offer advice on how to work the system to make a student more eligible (e.g., by hiding parents' income or advising them to move assets into the student's name). Both are unethical practices and should be avoided like the plague to avoid any hint of scandal.

Financial Aid Kickoff

Whether you're planning to offer financial aid assistance or not, there's a good resource available to help young students start the financial aid process. Twenty-nine states participate in College Goal Sunday, which takes place every February and is meant to help college-bound students fill out the paperwork necessary to apply for financial aid. According to the College Goal Sunday website, during the event students and their parents can:

○ Get free on-site professional assistance filling out the Free Application for Federal Student Aid form

○ Talk to financial aid professionals about financial aid resources and how to apply

○ Get information regarding student services available in their state

Even students who aren't sure they'll need financial aid are encouraged to attend, talk to the financial aid people, and get assistance filling out the forms. There's no charge to attend, and the event is usually held at numerous locations around each state. It's usually necessary for the family to bring a copy of their most recent tax returns to the session. For more information about College Goal Sunday, visit www.collegegoalsundayusa.org.

"There definitely are some sleazy people in this field who make the hair on the back of my neck stand up," says Sarah Soule, the Vermont consultant. "If you aren't ethical and committed to working with kids to make the right match, you don't belong in this business."

Be that as it may, there's no reason why you can't offer general financial aid advice, especially if you're a former director of admissions and financial aid like Whitney Laughlin, the New Mexico consultant, is. If you're new to the financing side, your learning curve will be a little steeper than that of someone whose business steers away from financial aid altogether.

The financial aid services most commonly offered by educational consultants are:

• Identification of funding sources/scholarship research

• Assistance with athletic and performing arts scholarship searches

• Assistance with financial forms and aid eligibility

Reaching Out

Some educational consultants choose to specialize in helping students of certain backgrounds or needs. For instance, Laughlin offers free pre-college workshops to Native American students through her foundation, Graduate Horizons. Massachusetts consultant Joan Bress is known for her work with performing arts students, while Arizona consultant Judge Mason has built a reputation for his expertise with at-risk students. Other student populations that can benefit from your expertise and compassion if you choose to specialize include learning-disabled students (e.g., those with ADD, ADHD, or dyslexia), and other nontraditional students like older adults, ESL students, second-generation Americans (particularly those who also are first-generation college students), and low-income students.

A Day in the Life

While no two days are alike for educational consultants (which certainly can make things interesting), there will be certain tasks you can expect to do regularly, if not every day, in the course of plying your new trade. They include:

- *Consulting with students and parents*: It's common for consultants to offer services by the hour or as a package that includes several meetings. These consults can take place in your home office, the student's home, or a neutral location.
- *Handling office administration*: This includes answering the phone, opening mail, handling accounts payable and receivable, and paying bills.
- *Purchasing*: You'll have to buy supplies for the business (e.g., office supplies, refreshments to offer during consultations, etc.)
- *Visiting college campuses*: You'll be doing this to observe, gather intelligence, and meet with college admissions officers, etc. (Later in the chapter we'll talk about this in more detail.)
- *Making travel arrangements for college visits*: Everything from airline and

> **Bright Idea**
> Writing a personal note of congratulations to your student clients after they've been accepted to the colleges of their choice will make them feel like a million bucks and will impress the parents, who will feel as though you really paid attention to their child. The result can be referral business for years to come.

Anatomy of a Consulting Program

While your slate of consulting services and the timetable on which they are delivered will be a very personal thing keyed to your particular interests, a typical admissions consulting package might look something like this:

Comprehensive College Selection Program

Stage I

○ Initial consultation (1 session): Describes the philosophy of the program and determines student and family needs

○ Assessment of academic and extracurricular performance (2 to 3 sessions)

○ Drafting of personal resume for the college selection process (1 session)

○ Completion of the personal resume during a student/parent conference (1 session)

Stage II

After one session to present the initial research list, additional consultations (as many as needed) for:

○ Paring down research to arrive at an optimum list of six college applications

○ Arranging itineraries for visits to college and university campuses

○ Networking with admissions personnel on the student's behalf

○ Determining whether the student and parents require need- or merit-based financial aid and assisting with the search for scholarship opportunities based on parameters stated at the conclusion of Stage I

○ Strategizing the essay and other subjective application elements

○ Assisting the student to meet deadlines for final applications

Source: James C. Heryer, *College Guidance & Placement*

hotel reservations to mapping your driving route using MapQuest or the auto club falls into this category.

- *Doing research*: Because you're not likely to have the time or the financial resources to visit all of the country's nearly 4,400 universities and colleges personally, you'll need to do most research remotely when you're starting out. You can use the internet to find out a lot about America's colleges, or you can write or call admissions officers for information. Also, once you get to know other educational consultants through professional organizations and campus tours, you'll be able to use them as resources, too.

- *Meeting with high school counselors*: Cultivate these professional relationships as a way to generate future referrals. Just be sure to assure them you're there to complement their services, not supplant them.

- *Meetings with parent groups*: Giving free workshops and seminars to parents of high school-age students on topics like "How to Fill Out a College Application" or "The Five Things to Include in a College Essay" can reap a lot of future business from folks who realize they really don't want to do all the college admissions work themselves.

- *Networking*: Hobnob with other professionals through organizations like the chamber of commerce, Rotary club, and other civic organizations to create another good source of referrals.

- *Pursuing professional development opportunities*: Courses and seminars like IECA's Summer Training Institute for Independent Educational Consulting can help you grow professionally and keep your skills updated.

Staffing Up

While most industry experts caution against hiring staff too early in the course of a new educational consulting practice, there's always the chance that you'll need some help managing your business, even if it's only to answer the phones while you're away on a college visit. A cost-effective way

▲

to get the assistance you need is to hire a college student to answer the phone, type, file, and do other light clerical work. Because of the nature of the work and the relative inexperience of a college-aged worker, you can pay minimum wage or perhaps a little more. Keep the total annual wage paid out under $600, and you won't be liable for payroll taxes, nor will you have to withhold taxes from the employee's pay. (Payroll taxes and other financial matters are discussed in more detail in Chapter 11.)

Of course, with today's technology, it's possible to pick up your messages just about anywhere, so you may never need to hire someone to help with the telecommunication tasks. But if you prefer to offer a higher level of customer service to clients who call in your absence, consider hiring an answering service, which will answer the phone using your company name. To find such a service in your community, look in the Yellow Pages or on yellowpages.com under "Telephone Answering Service." A real benefit of hiring this kind of service from a tax standpoint is that the company is completely liable for taking care of taxes, benefits, etc., for its employees. You just pay an hourly rate for the service. In addition, you'll get a professional level of service that may be lacking with a college kid who has never before held a job.

Perhaps the only other type of employee you may wish to hire one day is a tutor to help students who may need a little educational edge to make a good impression on college admissions officers. James Heryer, the Missouri consultant, employs four contract tutors who instruct on the SAT I and the ACT. Depending on the skill and experience of the tutor, minimum wage probably won't do for contract workers like these. At the University of Michigan, for instance, where there is a dedicated tutoring program, tutors are paid $8.75 an hour, while in the Littleton (Colorado) Public Schools district, reading tutors start at more than $20 an hour (and not surprisingly, they're required to have at least a bachelor's degree and a valid Colorado teaching license). If you decide you need a contract tutor or two on your team, you may wish to call your local school system to get an idea of how much schools are paying in your neighborhood.

Visiting Time

As you'll recall from Chapter 1, the first year of a new educational consulting practice can be mighty lean, financially speaking. The main reason for this is that your first 12 months need to be devoted heavily to making the rounds of college campuses to learn about their programs, their environments, and even their physical layouts.

"It takes at least a couple years to get established and work through the learning curve," says Steven Antonoff, the Colorado consultant. "You have to make visits and be out there on campus. After the first two years, good consultants are out four to six weeks a year making visits because that's the best way to keep up with what's going on."

Maryland consultant Charlotte Klaar agrees. "Always learn for a year before you work with someone for a fee," she says. "That's the only way you'll know what you're talking about and stay a step above those who do nothing more than buy a couple of books and think they're educational consultants."

College visits are so important that even established educational consultants continue to visit college campuses—and some of them more than once. Klaar estimates she has visited more than 500 campuses in her 10-year career, while Joan Bress, who founded her Massachusetts consultancy in 1999, makes a one-week site visit each month.

Bright Idea

If you run into price resistance when quoting fees, Sedona, Arizona, consultant Judge Mason suggests pointing out that your fee is just a tiny percentage of the $150,000 or more the client is about to spend on college tuition. In return, the client gets someone who knows colleges well and enjoys working with kids, and can direct them to the institutions where they'll be most successful.

She focuses on all aspects of the college experience, from the social to the academic environment, and along the way talks with admissions people and faculty to get a well-rounded sense of what the institution is like and what it offers.

"I eat a lot of food in college cafeterias and dining halls," Bress says with a laugh. "College visits are vital for success in this field, because without a real commitment to traveling, a consultant will be at a great disadvantage. There's really no other way to get to know the kids and the schools."

While Laughlin says she has personally visited 95 percent of the schools her kids have applied to because "it's something you can't do on a computer," it isn't necessary to visit every school that every student you counsel wishes to attend. For one thing, as Bress says, it doesn't always fit into her schedule to jump on a plane and make a site visit. When it's not convenient, she calls on her colleagues at IECA who either live near the college in question or have visited it. But, she says, "When I see trends, I make sure I go there."

To save money, a new educational consultant should try to schedule visits to a group of colleges in a particular geographical region. This is easier on the East and West Coasts, where there's a denser concentration of educational institutions in heavily populated areas. But even in the Midwest and the South, where colleges are farther apart, you usually can drop in on a few colleges located within a few hundred miles on a single trip. If you can drive to these institutions, you'll save a lot of money, even when gasoline prices are spiking. But flying is not out of the question if you're creative. For instance, Antonoff happens to live in one of United Airlines' hub cities and has put himself on the airline's email list to receive news about last-minute specials. Then he earmarks one weekend a month for travel—even though he may not know exactly

Beware!

Experienced educational consultants say that you should always have an upper limit on the number of meetings and hours your consulting package includes. You can always add on additional time at your hourly rate, if needed. But never give away your time—it's a commodity just like a product is, and as such it's worth charging for.

where he'll be off to until almost the last moment. "If an email comes across that says I can go to Seattle or Indianapolis for $69, for example, I'm there," he says.

One last way to visit colleges is by joining a college tour. You'll find information about tour opportunities in Chapter 7.

For What It's Worth

Figuring out what to charge tends to be a difficult task for educational consultants but not necessarily for the reason you might think. "Some people feel guilty taking money for consulting, partly because they never had help themselves when they were in school and they were perfectly fine," says Antonoff. "But as they develop expertise and realize how good choices affect lives of young people, they get over it and feel what they do is worth it."

Heryer concurs. "I worked hard to develop a professional edge and my time is valuable," he says. "I find that although people sometimes balk at my fee, once I get them in here and I develop a rapport with them they realize the value of what I do. Although some do take time to deliberate after we meet, a high percentage [of the people who contact me] hires me."

Charlotte Klaar has a pragmatic approach to rates. "I ask potential clients, 'Would you buy a house for $120,000 to $140,000 without a Realtor protecting your interests?'" she says. "Then I share my experience and qualifications with them, and [the fee is] no longer an issue."

It's possible to structure your rates in many ways. Some consultants charge an initial consultation fee just to sit down with the student and family, then deduct that fee from the cost of subsequent services. Others charge by the hour for services like college selection or forms completion, while 90 percent of IECA members offer packages of services. For instance, Whitney Laughlin offers a package that includes three appointments (each 60 to 90 minutes long), research time, career skills assessments, a list of colleges tailored to the student's needs, financial aid counseling (if requested), and more.

In some cases, you may find that one type of fee arrangement works better than others. Vermont educational consultant Sarah Soule says that charging by the hour works best in her area, which is right in the middle of the Northeast where many colleges reside. You may find that a similar situation exists in your part of the country. Talk to professional colleagues to get a take on what the market will bear.

Rather than settling on just one of these fee structures, it's usually better to offer a selection to potential customers, partly because some students will need more help and partly because some families won't know exactly how much help is needed and may have limited means. It will be up to you to suggest whether an hourly rate structure or a package deal might work better and be more cost-effective for the client.

> **Fun Fact**
>
> There are 12 schools in the United States that do not charge tuition. Five are military (the Air Force, Coast Guard, Merchant Marine, Military and Naval academies), while many of the other seven (including College of the Ozarks, Cooper Union, and Webb Institute) expect their students to work 10 to 15 hours a week in exchange for free tuition.

As mentioned in Chapter 1, an IECA survey showed that the rates charged by educational consultants range from $75 to $300 an hour, or an average of $140 an hour. Package rates range from $750 to $7,500, with an average of $3,200. Naturally, the area where you do business has a lot to do with how much you can charge. For example, you can't charge $300 an hour in a fiscally conservative community like Kansas City, but no one would bat an eye if you charged that much or more in Malibu.

Antonoff offers another suggestion for determining how much the market will bear. "If the going rate for a massage in your community is $85, you could probably charge more than that for educational consulting," he says. "Or look at the hourly rate of psychologists to get a feel for how much is possible."

Finally, while you may not be able to charge the big bucks when you first get started because you won't have enough experience yet, you should do a careful analysis of your personal needs and figure out how much income you need or want to make. As part of that analysis, factor in how much your growth plan—i.e., visits to colleges, professional development, etc.—will cost, as well as how much you want to work, and run some numbers. Ultimately the rate you charge has to be sufficient to enable you to meet your living and business expenses, put some money in the bank, and have some fun.

But whatever you do, make sure you charge for everything you do, advises Laughlin. "I don't do 'get-to-know-me' consultations for free," she says adamantly. "Have clients pay you by the hour, then fold the cost into a package when they hire you. You're giving them valuable information, so never give it away for free."

On the other hand, IECA does recommend offering a brief, no-charge introduction meeting, but executive director Mark Sklarow believes you also need a good follow-up strategy if you want to land the business.

"A new, freshly minted consultant called me recently and said she had followed all our advice about having a no-charge first meeting, but after she did five or six of them, she still didn't have any clients," he says. "My advice to her was to phone each family when no one is at home and say, 'I really enjoyed meeting Johnny, and I think I can help him. I just wanted to let you know my calendar is filling up.' Then I told her to hang up. The next time she called me, she said three out of the five had booked with her. Which just proves that people are undecided, and if you can connect with the family and be earnest about your interest in the student and what you can offer, you'll get the work."

Doing Your Homework

It's pop quiz time, class. Take out your pencils and checkoff the best answers:

1. When Coca-Cola launches a new flavor of Coke, do the developers just mix up a batch, taste it, like it, bottle it, and ship it off to party stores?

   ❑ Yes   ❑ No

2. Does General Motors auction off the right to name its new vehicle models on eBay?

❏ Yes ❏ No

3. Does Sears sell many iceboxes?

❏ Yes ❏ No

Pencils down, class. The correct answers are no, no, and no. That's because savvy manufacturers test their products, concepts, and even ads before any of them go to market. The idea is to identify whether the product, et al., will catch the public's interest (or in the case of the icebox, whether the product is still viable and useful), which is an indicator of whether consumers will be induced to buy.

Services like educational consulting also benefit from such testing. It's helpful not only to determine whether your target market will be interested in your services, but also whether there's even a need in the community where you're based, and other important factors. Toward that end, this chapter touches on the market research that will be helpful for determining whether your business will be viable and can prosper.

Studying the Market

One of the best ways to determine what the market thinks about your service is to do a focus group. Focus groups informally bring together people from a particular target market with certain desirable characteristics (e.g., household income of a certain amount, education level, etc.) so a researcher can ask questions related to the proposed service or product. The trouble is, the focus group process can be expensive. You'll need a script developed by a professional market researcher, and you'll need a place to meet (usually a room in a hotel or other public facility) and a facilitator. Add in the cost of the honorarium (and possibly snacks) necessary to induce people to participate, and you could be looking at thousands of dollars.

Beware!
Market research experts say that many new small-business owners either have no idea who will use their services, or they assume everyone will. Take nothing for granted—do your market research homework and analyze the results carefully so you have the best chance of positioning your business properly.

Educational consulting experts say it's possible to conduct both primary and secondary research that will yield valuable information without the high price tag. On the primary research side, direct-mail surveys are a particularly good way to obtain information. But we won't kid you—surveys can be tricky to write well, especially if you've never done one before. Rather than hiring a market research company, which probably will charge you a lot for such a small job, try asking any university marketing professors you might be acquainted with or call the marketing department at your local university for (affordable) assistance. If the professors are not willing or able to do the job themselves, they could assign the task as a class project instead, as marketing professor David Williams of Wayne State University in Detroit does.

Optimally, your direct-mail survey should be no more than a page and whenever possible should ask open-ended questions (i.e., those that require more than a yes-no answer). Experienced marketers also will tell you that enclosing a small financial stipend—even as little as $1—and a self-addressed, postage-paid envelope for returning the questionnaire will help to improve your response rate.

If you've ever studied consumer behavior or taken any marketing classes, you may wish to create your own survey. You'll find a sample direct-mail questionnaire on page 28, as well as a market research letter and response postcard, that you can use as a guideline.

Making a List

While your questionnaire is in development, you'll want to start looking for a mailing list you can use to sample your target market. There are quite a few list brokers that specialize in selling mailing lists to marketers like you. The cost is generally nominal (usually $50 to $185 per 1,000 direct-mail names, or up to $400 for email addresses), and the lists themselves are organized in categories by demographics so you can isolate just the people with the demographics in which you're interested. For example, one demographic that is likely to be of interest is education level, because, according to Mark Sklarow, executive director of IECA, people who are better educated are more frequent clients of educational consulting services. Other demographics that might be appealing include income level (obviously, people at higher income levels are more likely to be able to afford your services), geographic location (e.g., upscale or middle-class neighborhoods), and communities with a higher percentage of private and parochial schools. You may have to do a little preliminary primary research at the library or courthouse to determine exactly where these areas are.

Some organizations also make their membership rosters available for purchase. To find out whether there are organizations you'd be interested in contacting, visit your local library for a look at the *Encyclopedia of Associations* (Gale Cengage Learning). Or try a free trial of the *Directory of U.S. Associations* (www.marketingsource.com, 800-575-5369), which lists professional, business, and trade associations; 501(c) nonprofit organizations; chambers of commerce; and other community institutions. Finally,

▲

Direct Mail Questionnaire

Wendie Berry Associates
College Consulting

March 9, 20xx

Bonnie Stephens
13736 Liberal
Fullerton, CA 92838

Dear Ms. Stephens:

Do you have a son or daughter in high school? Then you've probably been thinking hard about the opportunities and options that will be available to your child after graduation. If those options include a college education, then you may already feel like the pressure is on to make the right decisions and choices. And talk about pressure—the decisions you make about college today will impact your child for the rest of his or her life.

It can be difficult to know where to turn for the right information and insight when it comes to the college admissions process. But I can help. I am a college educational consultant and financial aid advising professional, and I live and work right in your community. I know the local schools and how they're preparing your child for college. But even more important, I have insider's knowledge about the admission requirements and practices at many local and national colleges. This is knowledge that can help match your child to the college or university where he or she is best suited and will thrive—both steps for current and future success.

If you'll take a moment to fill out the postage-paid postcard enclosed with this letter, I'll send you a packet of information that will show you how an educational consultant can make the difference between college attendance and college success. (Alternatively, you can scan and email it to the address below.) In the meantime, if you have an immediate question about educational consulting and how I can help you, either now or in the future, please call me at (555) 555-5555. I'll look forward to hearing from you.

Very truly yours,

Wendie Berry

Wendie Berry, M.A.

P.S. If you respond by March 30, I'll also send a copy of my special report, *Ten Places to Find Free College Money*, at no charge.

15601 Northline Road • Chino Hills, CA 91709 • (555) 555-5555 • www.wendieberryassociates.com
Info@wendieberryassociates.com

Direct Mail Questionnaire, continued

Front of Postcard

From:

_____

_____

_____

Important! Be sure to fill this out!

BUSINESS REPLY MAIL
FIRST-CLASS MAIL   PERMIT NO. 5555   CHINO HILLS, CA

POSTAGE WILL BE PAID BY ADDRESSEE

Wendie Berry Associates
15601 Northline Road
Chino Hills, CA 91709

NO POSTAGE
NECESSARY
IF MAILED
IN THE
UNITED STATES

Back of Postcard

Tape Together Here

▲

Direct Mail Questionnaire, continued

Inside of Postcard

Fill out and return this postage-paid card to receive free information about how your child can succeed in college with the help of an educational consultant.

1. Number of children you have in:

   _____ 9th grade   _____ 10th grade

   _____ 11th grade   _____ 12th grade

   _____ elementary school

2. Names of schools they attend:

   _____

   _____

   _____

   _____

3. Do you expect to apply for financial aid?

   ❏ Yes   ❏ No

4. Do you believe your child will be eligible for scholarship money?

   ❏ Yes   ❏ No

5. Which colleges interest your child and you most? _____

   _____

   _____

   _____

   _____

6. What is your household income?

   ❏ Under $25,000

   ❏ $25,000–$40,000

   ❏ $40,001–$55,000

   ❏ $55,001–$70,000

   ❏ $70,001 and up

7. What is your profession?

   _____

   _____

   _____

8. Would you like to be contacted by an educational consultant?

   ❏ Yes   ❏ No

9. If yes, please provide a phone number:

   _____

10. Please provide your email address to receive updates on issues of importance to college-bound kids:

    _____

    _____

the *Standard Rate and Data Service Directory* (Kantar Media, http://next.srds.com) has information about companies that sell mailing lists and is usually available in libraries in large cities.

Because you're likely to be interested in reaching people in upper income brackets, you should have your survey printed on good quality paper. A quick-print shop like FedEx Office can handle the job at a reasonable cost.

Checking Out the Competition

Obviously, it's important to survey your prospects to find out what's important to them and what it will take to coax them into using your services. But a little primary research also is in order to determine who your competition is. "Look at the local market to be sure you're in a community that will support an educational consultant," Sklarow says. "Are there six consultants in your area already? If so, what will you do to differentiate yourself? Or if there are no consultants, will you have to spend a lot of time explaining what you do instead of doing your job? These are all things to consider." See the "Market Research Checklist" on page 32 to organize your efforts.

Speaking of your prospective competition, there's absolutely no reason why you can't take the direct route and speak to them one on one. Although there will always be those who will be reluctant to or downright unfriendly about sharing information, Sklarow says that many educational consultants—especially those who are IECA members—are happy to talk to aspiring consultants. So "find out what others say about the industry, what they do and what they charge," he says. "Take them to lunch and ask about their business and the state of the local public, private, and parochial schools. Then consider whether the economy is surging or stagnant and you'll have a pretty good idea of whether the area can support another consultant."

Joan Bress, the Massachusetts consultant, successfully used primary research to determine whether her business would be viable. "My market research consisted of talking with a lot of people, including college people, to figure out why students weren't graduating; people with college-aged children; and people who wished they had known about this business five years ago when their children were in college,"

> **Dollar Stretcher**
> The SBA has a wealth of free marketing information and tips on its website at www.sba.gov. For one-on-one assistance, contact one of SCORE's 364 chapter offices nationwide through its website at www.score.org. This SBA partner offers many free services and is staffed by working or retired business owners and executives who understand the challenges you face.

▲

Market Research Checklist

Use this tool to make sure you cover all the bases when it comes to investigating your target market:

Activity	Date completed
Conduct primary research	
1. Survey	
2. Interview educational consultants	
3. Conduct focus group(s)	
Conduct secondary research	
1. Internet	
2. Census Bureau (www.census.gov)	
3. Local government records	
4. Other	
5. Other	
Explore demographics	
1. Age	
2. Education	
3. Heads of household/families with high school-age children	
4. Income	
5. Survey: write, or find someone to write it	
Contact list broker	
1. Number of records required _____	
2. Mail survey	
3. Tally responses	
4. Analyze data	

she says. "This kind of informal research is necessary to see if the market can support the business."

Yet even though her research demonstrated that the business would be viable, Bress had a failsafe measure in place—just in case. "There are not that many educational consultants in central Massachusetts, so I didn't completely close my therapy business

Extra Credit

While your local market and your personal interests will dictate the scope of your market research efforts, Mark Sklarow, executive director of IECA, says it's helpful to ask certain questions and consider specific options when making decisions about how and where to establish your consulting business. The questions you might want to ask yourself include:

○ How affluent is the community where you intend to set up shop? What is the median income level?

○ How educated are its citizens? (Research shows that more educated people tend to use educational consultants.)

○ How many public schools are there in the market area? How many private schools? How many parochial schools?

○ Which type of school has the highest enrollment? (People who pay for their child's education may be more likely to pay for an educational consultant.)

○ How strong are the schools academically? What percentage of students goes to college?

○ How many educational consultants are already in the community?

○ How can you specialize to differentiate yourself from the others?

○ What is the state of the local economy?

before starting the consulting business because I wasn't sure it would actually work out," the former clinical social worker confesses.

While you're pondering the local competition, you can also start gathering secondary research. There's a ton of free information available at your local library and, of course, on the world's premier research tool, the internet. Reputable places to start looking for demographic information include the U.S. Census Bureau (www.census.gov), local economic development organizations, your local municipality (city, county, borough, etc.), and local utility companies, all of which keep information like census tracts on file that can be useful. The SBA (www.sba.gov) can also be helpful. Pull together an armload of this data, and spend a few hours (or maybe even a few days) analyzing it, and you'll have a good picture of what the local employment picture will be for you. In the meantime, there's a "Market Research Checklist" on page 32 that you can use to keep track of your research efforts.

On a Mission

As part of the fact-finding mission you've undertaken before officially opening your business, you need to write a mission statement. Marketing professionals recommend writing a mission statement just like the big corporations do as a way to focus your business and to figure out what you want it to be now and in the future. It's a simple exercise that can pay big benefits in terms of keeping you on track to achieve personal and financial success.

Basically, a mission statement defines why your company exists. It should touch on your motivation for establishing the business, your goals, your target market, and your plans for reaching it. It also should be inspiring, easily understood, and to the point, as in Pepsi's most succinct mission statement of its generation: "Beat Coke."

Your own mission statement will probably be somewhat longer. For instance, Sedona, Arizona, consultant Judge Mason's mission statement is "Helping families find settings where children can thrive," and he finds it so inspiring that he also uses it as a tagline on his website and other printed promotional materials.

Here's the edited version of an even longer mission statement from a fast-food joint you may have heard of: "McDonald's brand mission is to be our customers' favorite place and way to eat. Our worldwide operations are aligned . . . on an exceptional customer experience . . . . We are committed to improving our operations and enhancing our customers' experience."

Marketing consultants say a good mission statement should be somewhere between those of Pepsi and McDonald's—perhaps no longer than 25 words—while renowned management consultant Peter Drucker said a good mission statement should be short enough to fit on a T-shirt. But the bottom line is, you should use as many words as you need to inspire and motivate yourself.

A good way to come up with ideas for your mission statement is by starting with your vision for your business. Toward that end, try writing down several words and

> ## Smart Tip
>
> Tip...
>
> Traditional mailing lists are rented for one-time use only, although you can pay an additional fee to use the same list more than once. Brokers know how many times you use the list because they're seeded, which means they include names of people with the list company so they get a copy of everything you mail and can monitor usage.

phrases that describe your business, then select the three that are the most important to you. Next, select several words or phrases that convey what you'd like the customer to think about your business. Finally, come up with words or phrases that describe what you think about the company's image.

Here's how a fictitious educational consulting business, Wendie Berry Associates, might approach the task:

Description of the business:

- Insider knowledge of the college admission process
- Support and hand-holding for college-bound kids making the biggest decision of their lives
- "Matchmaker" for kids and colleges

What I'd like customers to think about me:

- Insightful and competent
- Genuinely care about kids and making the right choices
- Seriously experienced admissions advisor

What I think about my business image:

- Professional
- Willing to go the extra mile
- Concerned about more than just the money
- Interested in kids' lives and goals

Now, here's how this consultant could put those thoughts together to create a mission statement:

Wendie Berry Associates' mission is to be the educational consultant of choice for Santa Cruz-area college-bound students, delivering sound advice and guidance to students that is sensitive to their needs.

Smart Tip — Tip...

If you ask other consultants for advice, be considerate of their time and be prepared to pay for it. "It has taken me 25 years to learn what I know, and I'm willing to discuss it with others," says New Mexico consultant Whitney Laughlin. "But as a professional courtesy, you should send a check if you pick someone's brains."

Fun Fact

In the movie *Jerry Maguire*, the title character writes a mission statement that, at 30 pages, is more like a mission novel. He's promptly fired for rocking the company boat, which of course won't happen when you write your mission statement, no matter how long it is, because you're the boss!

Here's another one:

Wendie Berry Associates provides college admissions insight and support for high school students, matching them to the educational institution that will help fulfill their aspirations and positively shape their lives and future careers.

And here's a short one:

Wendie Berry Associates helps kids succeed academically, intellectually, and socially.

Are you ready to get inspired? Turn to the "Mission Statement Worksheet" on page 37 and try your hand at jotting down some ideas that you can transform into a mission statement you can live by.

Mission Statement Worksheet

A mission statement can really help you plot your direction, then stay the course. Try this simple exercise as a starting point for formulating a mission statement:

1. What is your vision for this business? Where do you think you'll be in one, two, and five years? _____

   _____

2. Why do you want to start this business? _____

   _____

3. What skills do you bring to the business? _____

   _____

4. What are three key words and/or phrases that describe your business?

   a. _____

   b. _____

   c. _____

5. What do you want your customer to think about your business?

   a. _____

   b. _____

   c. _____

6. What is your opinion of this business?

   a. _____

   b. _____

   c. _____

7. What are your economic objectives for the business? _____

   _____

Mission Statement Worksheet, continued

Mission Statement for

_____

(your company's name)

_____

_____

_____

_____

_____

_____

_____

_____

_____

_____

_____

_____

_____

_____

Lesson Plan
for Success

With the completion of your market research, you're ready to start laying the foundation of your business empire. Now, we know it's tempting just to get some business cards printed and start prospecting for clients. But as you know from counseling kids who are making decisions that will affect the rest of their lives, most ventures work better when they spring from a sound plan, and your educational consulting business is no different. So in this chapter, we'll cover the basics of writing a business plan, naming your business, selecting its legal form, and acquiring any necessary licenses—in short, everything you need to make your business official and more likely to succeed.

Planning Ahead

Did you ever hear the story about Jim Carrey, who, as a struggling stand-up comedian, wrote himself a check for $12 million to represent the amount of money he thought he would earn one day? This was way before he hit it big, and he carried that check around in his wallet for years as he worked his way up from stand-up comedy to the hit TV show *In Living Color*. Finally, he landed his first movie, *Ace Ventura: Pet Detective*, for which he was paid—you guessed it—$12 million. Now, we all know that simply writing down a goal doesn't make it happen automatically. But writing down your goals does make it more likely that you'll achieve them, mostly because you'll see the steps you need to take to make them happen. And that, of course, is the basic premise behind writing a business plan.

Your business plan basically is your barometer of success, as well as the roadmap you will follow to achieve your goals. As a result, it should outline your plans, goals, and strategies in clear and concise detail, and in present tense. You'll want to keep it handy so you can refer to it on a regular basis to judge whether you're reaching your goals and whether your strategies are working. If they are, then you can set some loftier goals. But if they're not, you may need to retool the plan so you can reach them. But perhaps even more importantly, your business plan should be adaptable so it can change to meet current challenges and opportunities in your market as they arise.

Because it's one more thing you have to do when you launch your business, you may be tempted to skip this step. But don't do it. "If you don't have a map, then you don't know where you're going," says Steven Antonoff, the Denver educational consultant. "Your business plan doesn't have to be elaborate, and it doesn't have to be perfect. But it does have to spell out specifics like goals, how

Smart Tip
Research shows that people who set goals and write them down are more likely to achieve them and find success. So in addition to creating a viable plan for your business, write down your personal goals for the business and refer to them often. Then as you achieve them, set new goals so you always have something worthwhile to reach for.

much time you'll spend on marketing, and how you'll corral your resources."

Every business plan should have seven major components: an executive summary, business description, market strategies, competitive analysis, design and development plan, operations and management plan, and financial factors. Here's how these components apply to a college admissions and financial aid consulting business:

- *Executive summary*: This is where you'll summarize your entire business plan. In it you'll include a description of the business (e.g., homebased admissions counseling for LD students, or general admissions/financial aid counseling for private school students), as well as a description of the services you offer, the legal form of operation (which we'll discuss in the next section), and your goals (like the number of students you'll counsel the first year, the number of college fact-finding trips you'll take, and so on).

- *Business description*: Here's where you'll give background information about both the business of educational consulting and your target market. As we discussed in Chapter 1, information about this industry is sketchy at best, but you can glean enough facts to write a credible description.

- *Market strategies*: After analyzing the market research data you compiled in Chapter 3, you can analyze exactly what you need to do to reach prospective clients and how you'll do it. You'll be writing a marketing plan a little later (see Chapter 8), so you can include details about the strategies you came up with in this section.

- *Competitive analysis*: As discussed in the last chapter, part of your job as a fledgling business owner is to determine how many educational consultants already operate in your target market area. That information will help you determine how to position your business and identify other potential competitors' strengths and weaknesses. If there's anything that makes you unique (your 25 years of experience in high school counseling, for instance, when the competition has less than that collectively), you'll want to note that here.

- *Design and development plan*: Here's where you'll note your goals and devise a strategy for attaining them. As you know from Chapter 1, the first year is often lean for a new educational consultant, so one goal you may set might be a timetable for acquiring enough business so you can quit your day job.

Healthy Savings

Many new small-business owners choose to be known as sole proprietors because it's the easiest kind of business to form, and because there's so little paperwork involved at tax time (you just file a Schedule C with your 1040 and *voilà*, you're done). But what some entrepreneurs don't realize is that sole proprietorship brings you another financial advantage: You can write off the entire cost of your health insurance coverage for both yourself and your family. This applies to medical and dental insurance, deductibles, co-pays, and any other legitimate health-care expenses you may incur. But there is a catch: You can only write off these costs if your business is profitable, which is why you may have to remain on your spouse's or significant other's insurance policy for the first couple of years until you start making some money.

- *Operations and management plan*: Because you're likely to be a homebased educational consultant with little overhead and probably no employees, your day-to-day operations plan may look simple. Putting it down in writing, though, will help you visualize what you need to do to keep the business running smoothly while you expend energy making it grow.

- *Financial factors*: No matter whether your goal is to work part time until you can afford to consult on a full-time basis, or to take the plunge into educational consulting as your only means of support, you should do a forecast as a way to keep your business on track and help you keep your financial ship on the right course.

If this is all Greek to you, not to worry. Free help is available from your nearest Small Business Development Center (found in the federal section of the Yellow Pages under the SBA or by logging onto www.sba.gov/sbdc). Another free resource is your local library, which is likely to have a wide variety of books or software packages that

> **Bright Idea**
>
> To gain experience fast, team up with an experienced educational consultant, as Sedona, Arizona, consultant Judge Mason did when he started out. After forming a partnership with his mentor, he paid her a set fee plus a percentage of his sales, then handled business she referred to him. The partnership was dissolved when she moved away—leaving him with a successful practice.

can help to make the writing process less onerous. Finally, IECA is a treasure trove of information for people transitioning to a career in educational consulting. The organization offers workshops and seminars that touch on issues like business plan writing. You'll find more information about IECA in Chapter 7.

The Fine Print

The next thing you should do after developing your plan is to select a legal form of business for your consulting enterprise. According to Mark Sklarow, executive director of IECA, educational consultants overwhelmingly choose to be sole proprietors, partly because they perceive their liability to be low and partly because it is so simple to form a sole proprietorship—basically, you select a unique name for your business (more on that later) and file an extra form or two with your taxes. If you're concerned about personal liability, however (as in what-if-some-clueless-parent-sues-me-because-his-son-didn't-get-into-Yale?), you may not be comfortable as a sole proprietor.

There are four legal forms of business you can choose from, including the aforementioned sole proprietorship, the partnership, the corporation, and the limited liability company (LLC). The main difference between them relates to the amount of risk you're willing to take. If you're not especially concerned about being sued (and it is fairly unlikely in this field, though not impossible), a sole proprietorship is probably best for you. If you want to enter into an agreement with another business professional (either another educational consultant or a counseling professional like a psychologist who specializes in family issues or crisis management), or you want to make your spouse/significant other a player in the business, then you may want to form a partnership. Just remember that with a partnership, each partner is liable for the other's actions, which sometimes can be problematic.

When it comes to protecting your personal assets against liability, a corporation or an LLC is the best way to go. Both a C corporation and an S corporation offer asset protection, while an LLC has many of the benefits of a corporation but is more flexible and requires less paperwork.

"Although our members tend to be sole proprietors, we urge them to establish an LLC, which is the simplest form of incorporation," says Sklarow. "Some people say that [incorporation is] not really necessary in this line of work, but you definitely will sleep better at night."

It's usually a good idea to consult with an attorney to decide which legal form is best for your personal situation. You'll find some pointers on how to find an attorney in the next chapter.

Naming Rights

The stage has now been set for you to make one of the most important decisions in your fledgling business's young life: selecting a business name. Because you'll be helping families make crucial decisions about the second most important thing they'll ever spend money on (a house being the first), you'll want to choose a name that's both professional and evocative of what you do.

It's very common for educational consultants to name their business after themselves—and not for reasons of vanity. "My name is my reputation," says Whitney Laughlin, the New Mexico educational consultant. "I named the business after myself because I wanted to sink or swim on my own reputation and hard work."

Similarly, Sarah Soule, the Vermont consultant, traded on her own name because of her previous experience with college admissions. "I have lived in Vermont the bulk of my life in a county with only about 100,000 people," she says. "I was already known professionally as an admissions counselor, so it was important to make sure my name was out there when I started the consulting business."

On the other hand, Massachusetts educational consultant Joan Bress had a very good reason for not using her name as the basis of her business, which is called College Resource Associates. "I wanted something that said what I did and I felt that using my own name didn't explain that," she says. "My name is already on my business cards, my stationery, and the articles I write, so it wasn't necessary to put it in the business name, too."

No matter which way you go, you'll probably want to evaluate a lot of different names before you settle on one. You might try brainstorming with friends or colleagues, as Bress did, to come up with a list of potential names. The Yellow Pages

> **Tip...**
>
> **Smart Tip**
>
> Banks usually require a copy of a small business's dba registration form as part of the process of opening a business checking or savings account, even if you're using your own name as the business name. Your business checks will then be issued with both your real name and your dba, as in "Robert Wittman, dba Wittman College Consulting."

and yellowpages.com also are good sources of inspiration, although you might want to try the online listings in another city far from your own so you don't select a name that's too similar to that of a local competitor. You can also use the "Testing Names" worksheet on page 45 to brainstorm names based on terms related to academics or other factors.

Testing Names Worksheet

Use this worksheet as a brainstorming tool for deciding on a suitable name for your new business.

List the word that comes to mind when you hear each of the following words:

1. Education _____   4. Consultant _____

2. College _____   5. Ivy League _____

3. Coach _____

List the top three characteristics that describe the type of work you do:

1. _____

2. _____

3. _____

List three of your city's, state's, or regional area's distinguishing features (like Nob Hill or Space Coast):

1. _____

2. _____

3. _____

Try combining elements from the above three sections in different ways:

1. _____

2. _____

3. _____

Testing Names Worksheet, continued

Still undecided? Then try mixing in any of the following terms related to university life:

• Semester	• GPA	• Class	• Senior
• Advisor	• Admissions	• Dissertation	• College
• University	• Campus	• Dorm	• Big 10
• Pac 10	• Ivy League	• SAT/ACT	• Academic
• Major	• Minor	• College prep	• Honors
• Liberal arts	• Graduate	• Higher learning	• Accredited

Did your name earn a perfect score? Then go straight to the head of the class. But first, test the name by saying it out loud several times to make sure it's easily understood, both in person and over the phone. Then do a preliminary availability check by looking through the local Yellow Pages or yellowpages.com before heading off to the county seat or other local government agency to apply for a dba. If you pass the availability test, the name is yours and you can order your business cards. Congratulations!

Making It Official

Once you make that momentous decision about your name, you have one hurdle left before you can order business cards. You have to register your business name with the appropriate local government entity (usually the county, borough, or parish). To register, you file for what is known as a dba, for "doing business as." This establishes that you are using a fictitious name for the business (even if it's your own name) and guarantees that your business is the only one in that geographic area that trades under that name. This is why, when you apply for a dba, the county will do a name search before it grants you the exclusive right to use it. Once the name has been cleared, it's yours to use indefinitely, although you will have to renew it every few years (generally three). If by chance the name is already taken, you'll

> **Bright Idea**
> If you plan to see clients in your home, try to provide off-street parking if at all possible, preferably in your driveway. Then be sure to keep the driveway and walkways shoveled in the winter in northern climates, and free of kids' paraphernalia the rest of the year. Risk management is always preferred over paying damages for slips and falls.

have to choose another one, which is why it's a good idea to come up with a couple of viable possibilities while you're brainstorming. The cost to establish and renew a dba is very nominal—usually only around $10.

One final thing you'll need before you put out your shingle will be a business license from the community in which your business will be located. In many communities, this is just a formality—basically local governments want to know that businesses operating within their boundaries (including those that are homebased) won't disrupt traffic, disturb the peace, or do anything hazardous or detrimental to the community. Local governments also like to keep an eye on their corporate neighbors because they're serious about enforcing zoning regulations. That's why you won't see a new business like an equestrian training center (aka horse farm) suddenly throwing open the barn doors in the middle of a suburban subdivision.

Business licenses usually are very inexpensive and are renewable annually. Because you may be seeing clients in your home office, you'll want to assure the official who issues the license that the business won't bring a surfeit of traffic to your street nor will police with semaphores and traffic cones be needed to direct customers to parking places. He or she will appreciate your cooperative and professional attitude.

Academic Advisors

As you can tell from the last couple of chapters, there's a lot of behind-the-scenes work that needs to be done to launch your new business properly. Chances are, among that work will be some tasks that, frankly speaking, you may not excel at, won't have an interest in, or won't have time for. So even though you may be operating on a shoestring budget in the formative stages of your consulting business, you really should seriously consider hiring a few business professionals to take on that less desirable work, particularly those tasks that relate to the law, accounting, insurance, or computers.

Did you just drop this book in shock? That's not surprising. Small-business owners—particularly those who haven't yet earned a thin dime in their new venture—often find it very difficult to part with their cash at the business's genesis, especially if they naturally excel at, say, reconciling the books or tinkering with computers and software programs.

But let's face it: There are only so many hours in the day, and it won't be long before you realize you don't have enough of them to counsel young people, visit colleges, and keep up on the latest tax codes (which change daily) or decipher all that incomprehensible fine print in service contracts. So cut yourself some slack and hire people who can help you with the administrative side of the business—namely an accountant, an attorney, and a computer consultant. (You also should have an insurance broker on the team, although strictly speaking you won't hire that person directly the same way you would hire these three other professionals.)

And by the way, there's an added bonus to putting these people on your team, either on a contract or hourly basis: They can help you avoid common startup blunders, which can include anything from not sending enough estimated taxes to the IRS, to leaving yourself open to liability claims. Finally, having business professionals in your corner makes your business look more stable and solid, which can be a big plus both in the eyes of those who wish to engage your services and to the community you serve.

Footing the Bills

Even if you've been doing your own income taxes with TurboTax for years, or you know your way around a profit and loss statement blindfolded, you still need an accountant for your business—if not from day one, then from the first day that you start making money. You probably know from experience that handling your personal finances can be time consuming, so just imagine how much effort you'll have to expend to manage your business finances, too. It just makes sense to put the whole job in the hands of a professional. "An accountant keeps me straight, which is good, because I have no clue about finances," says Vermont educational consultant Sarah Soule. "I have an accountant for the same reason a family hires me to help with counseling, not to mention he keeps me out of jail!"

Accountants are often small-business owners themselves, and usually charge by the job (like when preparing business taxes or making financial projections) or by the hour (like when balancing your books, sending out invoices, forecasting cash flow, or otherwise rowing your financial boat). It's not necessary to have an accountant on retainer unless you expect to do big business—which is highly unlikely in the startup phase of your business. Instead, look for a *numbermeister* who is willing to work with a small-business owner like yourself, whose financial needs are modest.

Your accountant's greatest value lies in his or her expertise in handling tax issues. The IRS issues new tax edicts frequently, and your accountant will keep abreast of those changes handily so you don't have

Bright Idea

If you find you don't have enough income at first to justify using an accountant, try managing your financial empire yourself by using an accounting software package like QuickBooks Pro (which is both comprehensive and user-friendly) or Sage 50 Complete Accounting. Both are available from office superstores, electronics stores, and computer stores, or you can buy them online.

to. He or she also can advise you about issues like setting up a simplified employee plan (SEP) so you can save for retirement tax-free, and will make sure those quarterly estimated tax payments mentioned earlier will be mailed or transmitted electronically on time (and in the right amount) so you don't incur costly penalties.

When choosing an accountant, it's usually best to choose a CPA rather than a public accountant. As you no doubt know, CPAs are college-educated, state-licensed professionals, while public accountants aren't certified and don't have to be licensed by the state in which they do business. Because of this, public accountants usually can't represent you before the IRS if (horrors!) you're invited

Dollar Stretcher

Need additional incentive to hire an accountant? Arizona consultant Judge Mason says that accountants know things you can't possibly know if you're financially challenged—especially when it comes to legitimate deductions. "Before I had an accountant, I never got a refund. After I hired someone, I suddenly got a huge refund," he says. That alone makes an accountant worthwhile.

in for an audit. Because you'll definitely want to have a friend on your side if that happens, it makes sense to pay a little more per hour and hire a CPA.

And speaking of rates, the amount you'll pay per hour or by the job will vary depending on the accountant's geographic location, education, and experience. In more general terms, that works out to about $68 an hour for accountants who offer bookkeeping services, according to a survey by Intuit. Alternatively, the U.S. Department of Labor's *2012–2013 Occupational Outlook Handbook* indicates that accountants earn a median rate of nearly $30 an hour. It's reasonable to assume a self-employed accountant may charge more—possibly $75 an hour or more.

Fortunately, there's a really simple way to keep your accounting costs down. Whenever you present your accountant with the records he or she needs to crunch your numbers, be sure to turn the material over in a well-organized package. For example, invest in a receipt-scanner like the Fujitsu ScanSnap or the NeatDesk so you can sort, store, and transmit your receipts electronically. Otherwise, take time to sort receipts into envelopes labeled "business expenses," "capital expenses," "charitable contributions" and so on, and keep accounts payable and accounts receivable documents organized by dropping them into their own folders. You also can use an accordion-style file that has been labeled appropriately to serve as your file box. Then turn the e-file, file box, or folders over to your accountant with a smile, because now he or she won't have to use billable time to sort your stuff into neat (read: usable) little piles.

To find the right financial pro for your business, ask your professional colleagues, your banker, or your local chamber of commerce for leads. Alternatively, you can call the American Institute of Certified Public Accountants branch in your state or log on to www.accountant-finder.com for a lead. It's best to choose an accountant who has experience with small-business owners, because he or she will be more likely to understand the challenges and intricacies of your business situation. In the meantime, check out Chapter 11 for additional bookkeeping strategies.

Lawful Pursuits

Because you are far less likely to know the intricacies of the law than you are to know how to keep your own books, the second person on your short list of professionals to hire should be an attorney. Mainly, you will need an attorney to draw up and/or review any contracts you give to prospective clients (see the sample contract on page 53), as well as to write the occasional letter. And of course, there's the outside chance that you may need assistance to protect yourself against lawsuits.

"We're hearing about errors and omissions cases more and more," says Mark Sklarow, executive director of IECA. "Some people are saying, 'We're going to sue because you didn't give us all the information we needed.' It makes sense to protect yourself."

"No one expects to be sued, but we live in a litigious age," says Joan Bress, the Massachusetts entrepreneur. "Have an attorney develop a service contract for you that says what you do, when you'll do it, and how much you'll charge, and be sure to indicate that your work is advisory and the results are not guaranteed. IECA also has a sample contract you can use to develop your own contract once you join the organization."

Sample Contract

JUDGE MASON
EDUCATIONAL CONSULTANT
WWW.JUDGEMASON.ORG
Helping Families Find Settings
Where Children Can Thrive

CONSULTING AGREEMENT

EDUCATIONAL CONSULTANT [JMEC] and _____ [herein referred to as CLIENT]. JMEC will provide CLIENT consultation for the purpose of assisting _____ [herein referred to as STUDENT], with the following PLAN[S]:

_____ Day School _____ Boarding School _____ Program School _____ Wilderness
_____ College _____ Summer _____ Psych Eval _____ Other

In consideration of such services by JMEC, CLIENT agrees to pay JMEC as follows:

[Check where appropriate]

_____ $xxx Initial Meeting and Analysis [counts toward any further fee[s] if I am retained as consultant]

_____ $xxx Per student School, College or Program Research PLAN.

_____ $xxx Wilderness Placement combined with School or Program PLAN.

_____ $xxx Wilderness Placement PLAN only.

_____ $xxx Residential Psychological Evaluation combined with School or Program PLAN.

_____ $xxx Residential Psychological Evaluation PLAN only.

_____ $xxx Summer Program Placement PLAN.

_____ $xxx Phoenix or Tucson Day School Placement PLAN.

_____ $xxx/$xxx Additional for each meeting in Phoenix/Tucson.

_____ $xxx Out-of-office daily fee for appointments in other locations.

_____ $xxx Travel [by air: FIRST or BUSINESS CLASS], meals, lodging

_____ $xxx Other _____

Full PLAN payment is due upon the signing of this Agreement unless otherwise specified. Interest of 1.5% or $15.00 per month, whichever is greater, will be charged on past due accounts. This contract is entered into in the State of Arizona.

150 Devils Kitchen Drive • Sedona, Arizona 86351 • 928-284-5719 • Fax 928-284-5802 • JUDGE@JUDGEMASON.ORG

Sample Contract, continued

CLIENT consents to the jurisdiction of the State Courts located in Arizona. CLIENT also agrees to pay all costs for collection including attorney's fees. CLIENT agrees to pay for travel, lodging and meals when these charges are incurred at the request of the CLIENT. These charges are billed separately and are in addition to the sums agreed upon as stated above.

When the above Services are selected, JMEC will provide STUDENT and CLIENT with information and related assistance to STUDENT and CLIENT in school or program selection and testing consultation. It is expressly understood that JMEC makes no representations or guarantees as to STUDENT'S chances of being admitted to any school or program, or of succeeding when admitted. For the paid PLAN fee, JMEC will assist in relocating the STUDENT during the first three months of attending their selected School, College or Program, if the SCHOOL, STUDENT and CLIENT feel it is necessary. However, if the STUDENT is DISMISSED or told that s/he must WITHDRAW at any time from the School, College or Program, and another type of School, College or Program is needed, JMEC will charge an additional fee for researching and recommending the other type of School, College or Program, if so requested by the CLIENT.

Entered into this _____ day of _____, 20 ___.

By: _____, JUDGE MASON, EDUCATIONAL CONSULTANT

AND CLIENT: _____   Total Amount: _____
                         [Please sign and return]

Amount Paid: _____ Date: _____   Balance due: _____

150 Devils Kitchen Drive • Sedona, Arizona 86351 • 928-284-5719 • Fax 928-284-5802 • JUDGE@JUDGEMASON.ORG

Of course, the best way to protect yourself is to establish a relationship with an attorney before you actually need one. Finding an attorney is easy—finding the right one can be a little more difficult. Your best bet is to look for a general practice lawyer who handles business or contract law, because—at least initially—the type of advice you'll need probably will relate to client contracts and letters of agreement. As with your accountant, it's usually best to engage someone who is familiar with small businesses so he or she will be more tuned in to the issues that are important to entrepreneurs like you. To keep the cost of said attorney down, look for someone who works in a small practice (one or two attorneys).

Legal fees can range from $100 to as much as $1,000 per hour. While you should definitely call or visit your attorney when it's necessary, keep in mind that you will be charged for every call he or she takes from you, as well as for every form filled out, every slip of paper filed, and so on. Because attorneys recognize that small-business owners' needs are likely to be modest, many offer startup business packages for $500 to $1,000 that include a few hours of time for handling basic tasks like incorporating

---

A Good Fit

Even though your contact with your attorney may be limited strictly to a phone call here or a form to fill out there, it's still important to find the right person who will meet your personal needs and expectations and be easy to talk to and understand. Obtaining a lead to a capable attorney from a trusted colleague will certainly help with the search, but there are questions you'll want to ask to judge whether you and your prospective legal eagle are a good fit—and whether you can afford his or her services. Some questions to ask include:

○ How long have you been practicing?

○ What's your area of expertise?

○ Do you have much experience representing small-business clients?

○ Will you do most of the work, or will a paralegal or other aide help out?

○ Is there a charge for an initial consultation?

○ What do you charge for routine legal work?

○ How can I reach you in an emergency?

or establishing an LLC, filing forms, and so on. This is usually enough for a consultant in the startup stage.

Because the work an attorney does for you is so important, you definitely should ask around for recommendations. Your banker, local economic development group, or even your county or parish government can be good sources of local leads. You can also find leads through an attorney referral service, which you'll find listed in the Yellow Pages or at yellowpages.com. Another good online resource is LegalZoom (www.legalzoom.com), which offers many legal services at reasonable prices.

Captain Cyber

PCs have revolutionized our lives, but they're complex and technical—and unless you want to spend your free time poring over incomprehensible manuals to figure out why you're suddenly confronted by the Blue Screen of Death, you need to hire a computer consultant for your business management team. Like accountants, computer gurus generally work by the hour, although some offer affordable maintenance packages that include services like installation of peripherals and memory, software installation, and general system maintenance. Generally speaking, it's a good idea to go for the package right away so you can be assured your system will keep running in top form. Then you can keep the consultant's number nearby for those unexplained computer glitches that require some by-the-hour work—a lifesaver in more ways than one.

"I could read the manual that came with my computer and software, but when you're making so much per hour and I pay my computer consultant less than that for something he can do in one-tenth the time, it's way more cost-effective to use him," says Whitney Laughlin, the New Mexico consultant. "He even helped me program my heart monitor!"

It's usually most practical to hire a consultant who will make house calls to service your equipment. This is a great timesaver you'll appreciate as your business ramps up and you don't have time to traipse across town on drop-off or pickup runs. In addition, an on-site visit saves you from perhaps the most frustrating task of all, which is unhooking all that spaghetti lurking behind your office furniture, and wrapping up the trailing ends so you can lug your equipment in for servicing.

Bright Idea

If you must unhook your computer equipment for a ride to the repair shop, use colored tape (the kind you find in the hardware store) to mark the male ends of the plugs and the female ports they plug into. This will save you a lot of frustrating hours when you put your system back together.

Your best sources for computer consultant leads will be professional colleagues or computer superstores, which often farm out the in-store work to their own network of consultants. Another option is Best Buy's Geek Squad, whose technicians make house calls and handle everything from computer hookup to operating system installation and support, hardware and software installations, and data backup or transfer. Rates vary by service. For instance, an on-site operating system installation is $230, while in-home virus and spyware removal is $300. Call (800) 433-5778 or visit www.geeksquad.com.

Risky Business

When you leave a job to make the leap to self-employment as an educational consultant, you gain a lot in terms of time, personal growth, and personal satisfaction. But you lose some things, too, not the least of which is the access to affordable insurance formerly provided by your employer. This, of course, is why the last member of your business management team should be an insurance broker who can help you acquire all the business and personal insurance you need.

The advantage of using a broker over an insurance agent is simple: Brokers usually represent many different insurance companies and as a result are able to present you with many more viable choices than would an insurance agent who works for a single company. This is important because you may find you can get a better price on your business insurance from one company and a lower cost on your other insurance needs from another. A broker can help you cut through the maze of insurance products efficiently and effectively. You can find brokers listed in the Yellow Pages or at yellowpages.com in the "business" subcategory of the "Insurance" listings, but of course probably everyone you meet will be happy to share the name of the broker they use, so ask around.

Types of Business Insurance

As you probably know, there's an insurance policy for just about any type of risk you can dream up. Of course, if you were to purchase coverage for every possible contingency, you probably would be working to pay for your insurance premiums and nothing else. So your objective when buying insurance is to figure out how much risk you're willing

> **Tip...**
>
> **Smart Tip**
> Even though a good attorney can draw up a written contract that should protect you from potential problems with students who think that hiring you is a guarantee they'll get into certain colleges, it's still a good idea to buy general liability insurance. Join an organization like IECA and the cost will be nominal—and worth it.

to take, then buy enough insurance to offset the risk that could force your company into bankruptcy or otherwise cause significant financial difficulties. Your broker can help you determine what types of insurance you might need to feel comfortably in control of your business life.

Among the types of insurance you may wish to consider for your new consultancy are:

- *General liability.* This is a must for an educational consultant, particularly if you plan to see clients in your home office. It protects you (and your employees, if you choose to have them) if you're sued for damages after a bodily injury on your property, as well as against property damage (like if you accidentally dropped a client's laptop or drove over some elaborate landscaping as you backed down a client's driveway). Probably the best deal on professional liability insurance is available through IECA, which offers liability insurance coverage at group rates. But of course you have to be an IECA member to take advantage of this benefit.

- *Errors and omissions.* This type of specialty liability insurance comes in handy if someone decides to sue you over a perceived error. According to Sklarow of IECA, the organization's general liability policy includes this coverage; otherwise, you can purchase this policy from any broker.

- *Business interruption.* If you suffer a loss due to a natural disaster, fire, theft, or other insured loss, this type of policy will pay the cost of your normal business expenses. Because your home office is the hub of your business and financial empire, this type of insurance is worth considering.

- *Equipment.* This one protects you against fire damage or theft of your business equipment and is a good idea if your homeowner's insurance policy doesn't cover it (and most don't). However, if you can add a rider to your current homeowner's policy, that should be sufficient to cover any loss so you won't need the additional policy.

- *Workers' compensation.* If you have regular employees on your payroll, you'll need this type of insurance because it's required in all 50 states. It covers them in case of injury or illness on the job, and the cost is based on the total cost of your payroll. By the way, as the owner of this business, you don't qualify for workers' comp, which of course is why you need your own insurance.

Types of Personal Insurance

- *Health.* If you're not covered on the health insurance policy of a spouse or a significant other, you'll need to obtain your own medical and dental insurance. If you quit a job with benefits to start your own business, your former employer is obliged to offer you COBRA continuation coverage for a period of 18 months. You should compare the cost against that of an entirely new policy before you sign up. You may actually find the new policy is less expensive.

- *Disability.* This type of policy can be a good idea if you're concerned about making ends meet in the event of a personal injury or illness. The policy pays a percentage of your gross income while you're recovering from a covered disability.

- *Life.* Important to have if you have a spouse, a significant other, or children who would need financial assistance in the event of your death.

- *Auto.* Yes, we realize you already have coverage on your personal vehicle. We bring this up as an FYI because auto insurance premiums are a deductible expense if you use the vehicle for business. Naturally, you can only deduct the part of the premium that relates to the business use of the vehicle (expressed as a percentage). However, you must make a choice between deducting the premium percentage or the actual mileage cost. It's usually a good idea to calculate both to figure out which one is higher.

You should think about buying business and personal insurance sooner rather than later to make sure you're protected adequately. To help you make some decisions, use the "Insurance Planning Worksheet" on page 60 to compare policies and premiums.

Insurance Planning Worksheet

Type	Required?	Premium	Annual Cost
General liability	no, but recommended		$
Errors and omissions	no		$
Business interruption	no		$
Equipment	no		$
Workers' compensation	yes		$
Health	no, but recommended		$
Disability	no		$
Life	no		$
Auto	yes; liability in most states		$
Other			$
Other			$
Total Annual Cost			$

Your
Hallowed Hall

If you're like many independent educational con-

sultants, you probably came to your new consulting business

by way of a job in academia. As a result, you're no doubt used to

having an established and at least marginally organized office

in a school building in which to meet with students, computer equipment that's serviced for you when it goes down, and a cafeteria you can retire to for a quick bite with your professional colleagues.

All that changes when you go solo, of course. But you can hire a computer consultant to help with those electronic glitches, and you can join professional organizations (discussed in Chapter 7) for social/professional interaction. So the only other thing you need now—besides clients—is a home office from which to run your educational empire. This chapter discusses the best way to set up that office, the equipment and tools you'll need to run it, and the tax and financial benefits of establishing a command center in your home rather than in an outside facility. You'll also find some tips on where to look if you find yourself in need of an office outside your home.

Home Office Basics

Good news: The cost to establish the typical educational consulting office is quite low—unless, of course, you're unable to rein in your enthusiasm for the business, like the man Arizona educational consultant Judge Mason knows who spent $45,000 establishing an office outside of his home.

Fortunately, you won't have to spend anywhere near that amount of money. In fact, it's pretty typical for educational consultants to start out with just a telephone, a pad of paper, a couple of pens, and some business cards. Add in a new computer, as Vermont consultant Sarah Soule did, and you could spend around $1,200 for the basics. But no matter what you spend, what's even more important is having a dedicated space to stash your stuff, both for the sake of looking like a legitimate business enterprise to the IRS (which, of course, will have a great interest in anything you do) and to your clients, as well as to have an established place in which to work every day. For this reason, it's strongly recommended that you set up a dedicated office, preferably in your home.

According to Mark Sklarow, executive director of IECA, 50 percent of that organization's members work outside their homes (usually because they haven't quit their day jobs), while 25 percent work from a home office and 25 percent do a combination of both. We're here to tell you

> **Tip...**
>
> **Smart Tip**
>
> Finances aside, working from home has additional benefits, as Joan Bress, the Massachusetts consultant, discovered. "You have to see kids during the times that work into their schedules, which can be after soccer or dance practice," she says. "Also, I can work on Sunday afternoon if I choose to without having to drive anywhere, and everything is in one spot in my home. A home office has many advantages."

that especially when you begin your new business, it's best to spare yourself the expense of renting an office and establish a home office instead. The reason is obvious. With a home office, your overhead will be substantially lower, which is important when you're starting out, particularly because it can take as long as three years to really get an educational consulting practice off the ground and in the black. Keeping your business costs down will help you to get to that point sooner. And of course, your commuting expenses and your commuting time will be zilch, both of which will be welcome to a new business owner. Finally, you'll be entitled to write off the cost of that home office (expressed as a percentage of the square footage of your home) as long as it's used strictly for the business (i.e., no kids playing Angry Birds on the computer!). Having this kind of deduction on your taxes can be helpful, especially when your business really takes off and you're suddenly a high roller in Uncle Sam's eyes.

To help you estimate your home office needs as you read through this chapter, use the "Equipment Costs" and "Startup Expenses" worksheets you'll find on pages 76 and 78, respectively, to jot down the costs of whatever you think you may need. You may also find it helpful to refer to the sample equipment costs and startup expenses shown on pages 75 and 77, respectively, for a fictional educational consulting firm, Wendie Berry Associates, which is a sole proprietorship with one employee (the owner) that's based in a home office. The costs shown for that company reflect the typical costs and low overhead of someone starting a business in this field. For comparison, we've also included sample expenses for a second hypothetical educational consulting practice, College Bound Consultants, that's based out of an office building, and as a result has higher overhead. This company also is a sole proprietorship (the most common form for an educational consulting business), but employs two people, including the full-time owner and a part-time contractor who answers the phone and does light office work.

Staking Out Your Space

Before we discuss the things you'll need to run your business, it's important to consider the whole issue of office space. You probably know a self-employed person who takes pride in the fact that he or she works from a desk in the corner of the family room, or on any flat surface in the house that happens to be free of clutter. We can tell you that's not the kind of work setup you want to have for your consulting business. Not only is it not very comfortable or efficient to work among the kids' crayon drawings,

Dollar Stretcher

Need to paint or re-carpet your new home office to make it fit to be seen by clients or even just yourself? The costs of those home repairs are deductible expenses as long as that room is your primary place of business. Even furnishings and artwork are deductible. Check with your accountant about any IRS-imposed limitations on office improvements.

stacks of books, or piled-up laundry, but it's also not very good for your mental health or for your image as a professional. In fact, if you plan to see clients in your home, there's no way around it: You must have a dedicated home office, preferably in a room that has a door and sufficient space for appropriate office furniture for yourself, and guest chairs and possibly a coffee table or work table for clients' use.

Smart Tip

If you live in an area of the country that's particularly dry (or the humidity level inside your home is low because of central heat), an anti-static chair mat might be a good investment to reduce static charges that can damage computer data. That type of chair mat starts at about $100.

While a corner office in your penthouse with a view of the city, plush carpeting, and a Jacuzzi would be great, the reality is you can work efficiently out of any space, no matter how small, as long as it's arranged appropriately and is out of the mainstream of your home's high-traffic areas. The ideal situation if you're planning to see clients in your home is to convert a spare bedroom located on the first floor or perhaps the den or family room into Counseling Central. Barring that, remodeling your basement into usable office space or turning a garage or loft above the garage into an office are feasible options. Having such a dedicated space will make you feel like the professional you are and will serve as a catalyst for you to get down to business every day, even when the sun is shining and a box of golf balls is calling your name.

But of course, not everyone can spare that much room in the family homestead. If necessary, commandeer a corner of a room that is not being used extensively, such as the spare bedroom (which must continue to function as a spare bedroom), and place your office furniture there. If that's all you can manage at first, go for it—just plan to meet your clients at Starbucks or some other public place where you can get comfortable and spread out a little for a short period of time.

Office Furniture

No matter whether you are fortunate enough to have room to spare for an office or you're double-dutying a room in your domicile, you need to have appropriate furniture for that space. No six-foot banquet tables, please—instead, spring for some real furniture that will give you the aura of success and competence. Fortunately, you can find good-quality office furniture at affordable prices at office superstores like Office Depot and OfficeMax. For example, OfficeMax sells a line of furniture called the Heritage Hill Collection, which has a cherry wood finish and runs $499 for a hutch and $699 for a 70-inch, double-pedestal executive desk. Add a lateral file for $249 and you have a complete, professional office setup for under $1,500. Use the desk and the hutch alone as a computer work center, and you will spend less than $1,200.

Home Turf

While many educational consultants prefer to set up client meetings in their home office or in a neutral location like a coffee shop or restaurant, some, like Whitney Laughlin, the Santa Fe, New Mexico, consultant, make it a practice to visit clients in their homes. "I go to clients' homes to get to know the family, their circumstances, and the milieu in which they live, which helps me understand them better," she says. "In addition, by meeting in their home the chances of them missing an appointment are slim. Plus there's no office overhead for me as well as no liability issues because you're covered by their insurance while you're in their home."

While Laughlin highly recommends this type of setup when starting out as a new consultant, she admits there are disadvantages—mainly the time it takes to drive from here to there. ("I have gone to the moon [if I added up] all the driving I do," she muses.) Still, she says, this is a personal touch clients like, so it might be something you should consider yourself as you establish your practice.

Naturally, if your startup budget is slimmer than that, you can find other types of serviceable furniture for much less at the office superstores and even at department stores like Target. A basic desk will run as little as $100, while a midrange desk will be about $200. A computer work center with a hutch and built-in storage that will require some assembly runs about $100.

When it comes to your chair, get the best you can afford—after all, you'll be spending a lot of time in it so comfort will be important. A basic office chair starts at about $75, while higher-end chairs in fabric or leather may run as much as $700 or more. Spend the money—it absolutely will be worth it. One feature to look for is an adjustable height control so you can raise your chair to exactly the right level for your desk, which can save you from problems with tendinitis spawned by using a mouse for extended periods of time.

Fun Fact

Want an executive desk worthy of the consulting mogul you plan to be? Then the Dominic Gerard "Resolute" desk is the one for you. This replica of the desk presented to President Rutherford B. Hayes by Queen Victoria in 1880 (and still used in the Oval Office) is made of dark red mahogany solids and retails for $15,000.

Other items you'll need for your office may include a two-drawer letter-size file cabinet ($40 to $100 each), a four-shelf bookcase ($70), and a printer stand ($129 and up). Guest chairs run $100 and up, and it's often possible to get them to match your furniture. A chair mat to protect your hardwood floor or carpeting is also helpful if your office chair is on casters, and starts at about $50.

If you're really budget-minded, consider buying used furniture. Thrift stores often have good-quality furniture for sale—and sometimes it looks practically brand-new. The local newspaper classifieds can be a source of used furniture, as can the online auction house eBay and online classifieds like Craigslist. But beware when you're bidding online. People who sell large items like desks usually expect the buyer to pick up the item in person because shipping it would be cost-prohibitive. So be sure to check out where the item is located before you bid, so you don't win a beautiful antique roll-top desk from a seller in the Wolverine Lake area of the Yukon, Canada, when you're located in Wolverine Lake, Michigan. And there's plenty to pick from on eBay. A recent search for desks on the site indicated that there were more than 96,000 listings, ranging from a new Euro-style aluminum and glass model for $300 (with free shipping, so it probably requires assembly) to a U-shaped computer desk with hutch for $629.95 (plus $100 to ship it). The highest-priced item at the time was a nine-piece bird's eye maple-inlay office suite with a desk, hutch, and bookcase for $12,999 (and this seller will ship this one to you free).

Computer Equipment

While office furniture is important, if you had to select the one item that is of paramount importance to you as an educational consultant, it probably would be a computer. If you already have a working computer you can use strictly for the business, there's no need to buy a new one right away. But if yours is a dinosaur (i.e., more than five minutes old), you might want to fork over the cash, because it can be just as expensive to upgrade an older model as it is to buy a new one.

Unless you need graphics capability to design your own promotional materials (such as brochures and publications), you can buy lower-priced equipment and have all the power you need. For example, at the time of publication, Best Buy was offering the XPS x8500 computer with a 24-inch

> **Dollar Stretcher**
>
> Extra-large computer monitors are easier on the eyes than standard models, and are very affordably priced. A 24-inch HD wide-screen monitor is only about $170 at an office superstore, while a more space-friendly 20-inch monitor can be found on sale for as little as $99 at office supply and electronics superstores.

monitor and 8 GB of memory for $870. (The price goes up if you add more memory or a faster processor.) Then add on a printer like the HP LaserJet Pro M275 network-ready, wireless, all-in-one printer ($199) and you'll be good to go.

Additional accessories and peripherals you may find handy include a flash drive (as low as $10 for 8 GB of memory), a scanner (starting at $100), a mouse pad ($3 and up), and a surge protector for each of your peripherals ($15 to $50).

Finally, because you may be on the road a fair amount of the time (especially if you don't have enough room in your home for an office where you can entertain clients), you may want to invest in a laptop computer instead. As with desktop models, you get a lot for your money with laptops, and deals abound. For example, Best Buy recently offered a Toshiba Satellite 15.6-inch laptop with 4 GB of memory and a 320 GB hard drive for a paltry $299.99. Another recent deal was for an Inspiron 15z Ultrabook with a 15.6-inch high-definition screen, backlit keyboard, display touch screen technology, and optical drive (for reading and writing DVDs) for $750.

If you prefer a Mac over a PC, prepare to pay much more. A MacBook Pro with a 13.3-inch display, 8 GB of memory, and 128 GB of flash storage starts at around $1,600 and usually doesn't include a DVD/CD in the price.

Software

There are really only a couple of software packages that you're likely to need to run your business. The mostly widely used office productivity package is Microsoft Office Professional, which you probably know includes a suite of programs, including Word, Excel, PowerPoint, Access, Publisher, OneNote, and Outlook. One built-in feature that makes the Word suite so powerful is its document templates. The program comes with dozens of built-in templates, plus you can connect to Microsoft Office Online at http://office.microsoft.com to access hundreds more.

Office Professional 2013 retails for $400 and can be purchased at office and computer superstores.

Even if you hire an accountant, you'll probably want to keep track of your receivables and other financial data just so you know how your business is faring at any given time. Probably the best software to use for this purpose is QuickBooks Pro, which retails for around $250. Its ease of use and ability to interface with other financial programs like TurboTax makes QuickBooks a good choice for even the mathematically challenged.

Another option is Sage 50 Complete Accounting. It, too, handles standard accounting tasks like general ledger entries and accounts receivable/payable, and has analysis and reporting features. It retails for around $369 for a single-user license.

One last type of program you may find useful, especially if you are a techie, is scheduling software. This type of program allows you to schedule and keep your appointments electronically, and some programs synchronize with Outlook Calendar. You'll find the names of a few companies that sell scheduling software in the Appendix.

Fax Machine

With email, BlackBerry phones, iPhones, and texting, fax machines aren't quite as sexy as they used to be. But if you prefer not to open attachments, which can contain viruses; you expect to send and/or receive a lot of documents (like essays or applications that need a once-over before they're mailed); or you don't want to leave your computer on 24/7 in case a fax comes in, a stand-alone fax machine may still be a good idea for your business. Fax machines are very affordable at about $60 for a plain paper version or as little as $90 for multifunction models that fax, copy, print, and scan.

Telecommunications Devices

It's certainly easy to stay connected these days, thanks to the multitude of information management devices on the market, from that old standby, the humble telephone, to the iPhone. Most people can't live without at least a couple of them—and no doubt that will include you, too. Your choices include:

- *Landline.* You may be surprised, in this age of wireless communication, to see the lowly landline at the top of the telecommunication list. But despite the convenience of carrying your business phone with you everywhere you go, a serious business professional still needs a true professional office phone. A business phone will give you better sound quality and will have necessary features like a hold button, conferencing, and speakerphone capabilities. You'll probably often be taking notes while you're on the phone, so you should consider buying a headset-ready model; otherwise, you'll need to buy an amplifier (which costs about $200 or more) if you ever want to hook up a headset ($150 and up) to your phone. Polycom makes a line of full-feature professional business phones at many price points (available from Hello Direct and office superstores). Otherwise, a standard two-line speakerphone with auto-redial, memory dial, mute button and more will come in at $40 to $150.

Bright Idea

There may be no better way to make a classy impression on a client than by using a really great pen. A beautiful Waterman ballpoint pen, one of the world's finest, costs only about $120 retail (although an exceptionally fine fountain pen can cost $450 or more). But there are bargains to be had on online auction sites like eBay.

Voice-over-Internet-Protocol (VoIP) phone service can be a good choice for consultants who will serve students from coast to coast, so you'll need a VoIP-enabled phone to access the service. Hello Direct, Amazon, and Best Buy, to mention just a few, all carry these specialty phones. Alternatively, a VoIP service like Vonage can be accessed using your own business phone with a VoIP networking router, which connects the line(s) to your pre-existing DSL or high-speed cable service. See vonage.com for more information.

- *Cellular phone.* If you already have a cell phone for personal use, get a second line to serve as your business phone. Seriously. Don't try to start a new business and manage your entire life with one phone. The monthly service charge for an unlimited talk and text plan is about $90.

Cool phones abound, but the gold standard is still the function-rich iPhone, which runs about $199 for the 16 GB unlocked model with a new cellular contract. (The iPhone 5 runs $649 without a new contract.) As with any cellular phone, you'll pay a service activation fee of about $35, plus standard monthly access fees.

- *BlackBerry.* Considered to be the original "corporate image" phone, the BlackBerry Bold starts at around $100 and tops out at nearly $2,000 for

Smart Tip

If you're planning to install a new landline to use as your primary business line, you definitely should pay for an unpublished listing for your existing residential line. Excluding your home number from the phone listings will keep you from wading through dozens of business calls on your voice mail or answering machine to get to your personal messages.

the sleek BlackBerry Porsche Design smartphone. But if you'll be purchasing your phone on Planet Reality, plan to spend about $199 for a fully-featured model. You'll also pay an activation fee and a monthly access rate of $40 or more. For more information about BlackBerry, visit www.blackberry.com.

- *Answering machine.* Voice mail has all but sent answering machines to Communication Heaven, but there are those among us—particularly those of us who like to screen calls—who still favor this tried-and-true technology. A basic answering machine is only about $40.

Point-of-Sale Equipment

Consulting fees can add up fast, so your clients will appreciate being able to pay with plastic. You have three options for offering credit: using standard point-of-sale (POS) equipment (which includes a POS terminal and a receipt printer), using a POS software package on your computer, or using a mobile device POS application. Because you'll never have a college consulting storefront, your best (and least expensive) option is the mobile processing system. It consists of a credit card reader that attaches to or plugs into a smartphone, and a processing app. You simply swipe the customer's credit card through the reader and obtain a credit approval.

The system requires a merchant account to process payments, for which you'll pay a couple of fees (including a transaction fee of around 2.7 percent or less). Unlike standard merchant accounts, however, the mobile providers generally don't charge monthly service or setup fees, which makes them more affordable. The credit card reader is usually free, as well. Mobile POS providers to check out include Intuit GoPayment, PayPal, and USBSwiper, all of which offer merchant accounts as part of their service. You'll find contact information for each of these in the Appendix. And incidentally, you can get a POS system for iPad if that suits your needs better.

Copy Machine

Though a real convenience, a copy machine is not an absolute necessity, particularly because there's probably a quick print shop like FedEx Office near your home. But they are handy to have, especially now that personal copiers, which fit on a desktop, are only about $150. A stand-alone copier (which usually has a pretty

> **Bright Idea**
> If you'd like to accept electronic payments but wish to sidestep point-of-sale processing, consider using PayPal. Your client simply issues a money transfer to your PayPal account or your email address. You'll pay a fixed percentage on each sale, which you can certainly pass on as a fee to your client. For more information, see www.PayPal.com.

big footprint—possibly too large for your home office) runs $2,500 or more, but it can make double-sided copies, collate, sort, staple, and do other office tricks. Toner cartridges for desktop models sell for about $50 and up.

Office Supplies

We'd be willing to bet that, like most people, you have enough notepads, pens, paper clips, and file folders to open your own office supply store if this educational consulting thing doesn't work out. The point is, you probably won't need to run out to the office supply store to stock your desk. However, if somehow you managed to avoid the lure of the back-to-school product sales all your life, you might need about $150 for basic office supplies like copy paper (usually $25 to $50 for a case of 10 reams), copier toner cartridges, and a good-quality pen and pencil set. (Please, no 15-cent Bics when you're counseling kids who are poised to spend $30,000 a year on tuition!) Once you have what you need to get started, it's reasonable to assume you might spend about $30 a month on supplies as they run out, although there will be the occasional higher-priced purchase, like printer cartridges (around $80) and fax cartridges ($30 to $90).

Business Cards and Stationery

Judge Mason says he didn't get around to buying business stationery until he was in business for five years. Even so, it's a good idea to have professionally printed letterhead and envelopes for when you need to communicate with students and parents, as well as a professional-looking business card. You can expect to pay about $150 at FedEx Office or a stationery shop to have stationery and matching envelopes printed. If you're so inclined, shop online for a business printer and you may be able to save some money. You'll find a few sources you can check out in the Appendix.

Service Brochures

It's a good idea to have a general services brochure printed that you can distribute at high school events, chamber of commerce meetings, and anywhere else people—especially those with high school-aged children—congregate. A simple three-panel color brochure that lists your services and contact information will suffice. Expect to pay about $300 for 250 brochures.

Postage

While it may seem old school, you may find it necessary to mail the occasional brochure or other materials to prospective students and parents using Ye Olde Postal

Service. To cover any contingency, you should earmark some cash for stamps in your startup budget. It's so easy to purchase postage online, you might also consider buying a postal scale so you can cut out the middleman (the USPS clerk) and weigh and stamp up from the comfort of your home office. A super accurate digital scale costs only about $50 at office superstores. You'll find a list of online postage providers in the Appendix.

Services

Another startup expense you'll encounter relates to the activation of all the technology you'll be using. To begin with, you'll pay a $40 to $60 telephone line installation fee for a business telephone landline and about $150 to $400 per line for small-business phone service. That's a pretty big chunk of your monthly operating income, so it will probably come as no surprise that many sole proprietors choose to install a second residential line in their home rather than a business line. Educational consultants report that most of their business comes from referrals and word-of-mouth, so it's not necessary to have a published number in a phone directory. You may also have to pay an activation fee for your cell phone.

As for internet service, depending on what type of provider you have, you may have to pay an installation fee. Check with your provider for guidance. In addition, all of these services have monthly usage fees. See Chapter 11 for a list of typical charges.

> **Smart Tip**
>
> In real estate parlance, office space is classified as A, B, or C class. Class A properties were built after 1980, are 100,000 square feet or larger, and are in a business district. Class B properties are smaller, older (though renovated), and in good locations. Class C buildings are much older, haven't been renovated, and are in fair condition.

Vehicle

At last—something you probably won't have to run out and buy, assuming, of course, that the car or SUV you currently own is in good repair and reasonably attractive. (No 1979 Yugos need apply!) As you may recall from the last chapter, business travel expenses, including the cost of gasoline, oil changes, parking fees, tolls, and yes, your car payment, are all deductible expenses. But beware: If your vehicle does double duty as a business and a personal ride, then you can only deduct the percentage of the vehicle cost and expenses that relate to the business. For this reason, be sure to keep all receipts, and start logging your mileage in a logbook that you carry in your vehicle at all times. (You can pick up a pocket-sized auto mileage log at an office superstore.) If you don't plan to itemize all those expenses in terms of a percentage, you can still take a deduction for the miles you actually drive, as well as for parking fees and tolls. In 2013, the IRS allowed a standard mileage rate of 56.5 cents, but that figure is always

Fair Share

If for some reason you truly can't work out of your home—perhaps it's just too small, there's no parking for clients, your dog is exceptionally large and likes to shed on visitors, etc.—you may have no other option than to establish an office away from home. But if traditional office space is too expensive for your startup budget (likely), you should consider renting a small one-room office in an office building. For a monthly fee, you can rent a fully furnished business office (usually 500 square feet or less) in an office building with a receptionist, telephone answering service, conference room, and other business amenities—including that all-important business mailing address to which you can direct clients and mail deliveries. Many such rentals also come with access to other business services like administrative support, photocopying, and videoconferencing. The cost of these services is usually far less than hiring your own staffers or buying your own equipment.

If you will need office space only occasionally to meet with students and their parents, you may find it more cost-effective to rent space on a per-use basis instead. There are companies that rent office space to small-business owners like you on a per-use basis—say, for just a few hours or for a day here or there. This type of setup is known as "hoteling" (as in checking in and out whenever you need to), and the space is available by the hour on a first-come, first-served basis. These resource-sharing situations sometimes also come with the same types of add-on administrative services you'll find in a shared office space, but the services are often more limited. To find office-sharing companies, check the Yellow Pages or yellowpages.com under "Office & Desk Space Rental Service."

changing, so be sure to check with your accountant or verify it on the IRS' website at www.irs.gov. For additional information on business expense deductions, refer to IRS Publication 463, "Travel, Entertainment, Gift and Car Expenses," which can be downloaded from www.irs.gov.

Mail Call

These days it's a good idea to safeguard personal information like your home address, so you may wish to consider renting a post office box or a box at a mailing center like Mail Boxes Etc. This is an especially good idea if you don't intend to see clients in your home—then there's no reason at all to publish your home address anywhere. Having a post office box also is helpful for keeping your business mail separate from your personal bills and junk mail. The cost is about $60 for six months at the post office, or about $10 to $20 a month, depending on the size of the box, at a commercial mail center like Mail Boxes Etc. or the UPS Store.

Adding It Up

If you have been noting your anticipated expenses on the "Startup Expenses" worksheet on page 78 as you read through this chapter, you now should have a pretty good idea of what it will cost to launch your educational consulting business. Chances are, you can handle the cost with plastic or a cash withdrawal from your bank account. But if you do need some financial assistance because you've chosen to rent an office space or you intend to buy top-of-the-line equipment and furniture, you can find information about financing options in Chapter 11.

Going Off-Site

We know there's always the chance that you'll really want to open your business in an office suite or other off-site location. Office space is rented by the square foot, and the price depends on where you're doing business. According to OfficeFinder.com, an office space information and referral site, the average executive office is 120 square feet. To get an idea of how much 120 square feet of office space may cost in your market, check out the "Market Information" link under "Quick Office Links" at www. officefinder.com, which directs you to a variety of information sources. As you might expect, office space rates vary widely by geographic location. To get help finding the right office space, look in the Yellow Pages or go to www.yellowpages.com to search for a commercial real estate broker, or call the management company of any office building you're interested in. However, before you take the plunge, consider the advice of Steven Antonoff, the Denver educational consultant, who purchased a 1,000-square-foot office condo for his business. He says, "Never get an office immediately for this sort of business. It takes a long time to get enough income to afford it."

Sample Equipment Costs

Item	Wendie Berry Associates (Low)	College Bound Consultants (High)
Office Equipment		
Computer, printer		$ 2,000
Laptop, printer	$ 950	
Software:		
Microsoft Office	$ 400	$ 400
QuickBooks Pro	$ 250	$ 250
Surge protector	$ 15	$ 30
Multipurpose fax/scanner/copier		$ 90
Copy machine	$ 150	$ 1,000
Phone	$ 50	$ 300
Cell phone		$ 199
Answering machine	$ 40	
Postage scale		$ 50
Calculator	$ 10	$ 10
Office Furniture		
Desk	$ 100	$ 400
Chair	$ 100	$ 200
File cabinet(s)	$ 40	$ 80
Bookcase(s)	$ 70	$ 140
Chair mat		$ 100
Office Supplies		
Business cards, stationery	$ 200	$ 200
Service brochures	$ 300	$ 600
Miscellaneous supplies (pens, folders, etc.)	$ 100	$ 150
Computer/copier paper	$ 25	$ 25
Extra printer cartridges	$ 50	$ 50
Extra fax cartridges	$ 30	$ 90
Extra copier toner		$ 90
Mouse pad	$ 3	$ 6
Total	**$2,883**	**$6,460**

Equipment Costs Worksheet

Item	Cost
Office Equipment	
Computer, printer	$
Laptop, printer	$
Microsoft Office	$
QuickBooks Pro	$
Surge protector	$
Multipurpose fax/scanner/copier	$
Copy machine	$
Phone	$
Cell phone	$
Answering machine	$
Postage scale	$
Calculator	$
Office Furniture	
Desk	$
Chair	$
File cabinet(s)	$
Bookcase(s)	$
Chair mat	$
Office Supplies	
Business cards, stationery	$
Service brochures	$
Miscellaneous supplies (pens, folders, etc.)	$
Computer/copier paper	$
Extra printer cartridges	$
Extra fax cartridges	$
Extra copier toner	$
Mouse pad	$
Total	$

Sample Startup Expenses

Item	Wendie Berry Associates	College Bound Consultants
Mortgage/rent (first six months)	$0	$0
Office equipment, furniture, supplies	$2,883	$6,460
Business licenses	$20	$20
Phone (line installation charges)	$40	$40
Post office box (first six months)	$0	$120
Employee wages and benefits (first six months)	$0	$300
Startup advertising	$200	$200
Legal services	$200	$200
Vehicle	$600	$600
Insurance (annual cost)	$500	$500
Market research	$250	$250
Membership dues	$300	$300
Publications (annual subscriptions) and books	$50	$50
Online service	$25	$25
Website design	$800	$800
Web hosting, domain name	$80	$80
Subtotal	$5,948	$9,945
Miscellaneous expenses (roughly 10 percent of subtotal)	$590	$990
Total	$6,538	$10,935

Startup Expenses Worksheet

Item	Cost
Mortgage/rent (first six months)	$
Office equipment, furniture, supplies	$
Business licenses	$
Phone (line installation charges)	$
Post office box (first six months)	$
Employee wages and benefits (first six months)	$
Startup advertising	$
Legal services	$
Vehicle	$
Insurance (annual cost)	$
Market research	$
Membership dues	$
Publications (annual subscriptions) and books	$
Online service	$
Website design	$
Web hosting, domain name	$
Subtotal	$
Miscellaneous expenses (roughly 10 percent of subtotal)	$
Total	**$**

7

Schooled for Success

With all this talk about educational consulting and helping young people achieve their personal potential, we haven't yet touched on the educational opportunities that can make you a more effective consultant. Now, we're not necessarily talking about going back to your favorite hallowed halls for more sheepskins, although that's always a possibility if you're so inclined.

Rather, we're referring to the educational resources available through professional organizations, publications, and other means. Keeping abreast of developments in your field through these channels is important to your development as a small-business owner—or, as auto pioneer Henry Ford put it, "Anyone who stops learning is old, whether at 20 or 80."

Here are some resources that can help keep you young. Look in the Appendix for contact information.

Industry Associations

Whether you have decades of experience as a counseling professional or far less, you'll find that membership in professional associations can be very helpful, both in the resources they offer and the support they provide. They also lend you credibility in the eyes of your clients. "But the greatest value of professional associations and summer institutes lies in networking with other educational consultants," says Steven Antonoff, the Denver consultant. "Services are now spoken about openly and fees are online, so you can ask about anything, including what to charge."

"I personally would not hire an educational consultant [who] is not in IECA [the Independent Educational Consultants Association]," adds Sarah Soule, the Burlington, Vermont, consultant. "You have to go through so many hoops to get in that you know the members are committed, ethical, and knowledgeable."

Among the organizations whose hoops you may wish to jump through because they're so useful to educational consultants are:

- *The College Board.* Founded in 1900, this not-for-profit association is really designed to help students achieve college success and provide opportunities. But you'll find it useful because of its connection to more than 3,800 universities and colleges, 23,000 high schools, and 7 million students and their parents. It offers programs and services in admissions, assessment, financial aid and more, one of the best known being its SAT program.

Stat Fact

The College Board website (www.college board.com) has a wealth of useful information for educational consultants. For instance, a recent College Board report indicated that the average annual college tuition at four-year private non-profit institutions was $28,500 in 2011–12, vs. $8,244 for four-year public institutions.

Membership is limited to higher education institutions, secondary education institutions, and nonprofit associations, but you can find a lot of useful information for free on its site at www.collegeboard.com.

- *Higher Education Consultants Association (HECA).* This valuable resource for college admissions consultants was founded in 1997 to support those who assist students and their families with the options and opportunities found in higher education. In addition to inclusion in a searchable website membership directory, membership provides access to college-related publications, seminars, and an annual conference; marketing tools, and access to discounted liability insurance. A bachelor's degree or higher and experience in educational counseling are required to join. Annual dues are $200. For more information, visit www.hecaonline.org.

- *Independent Educational Consultants Association (IECA).* This nonprofit association represents only full-time and experienced independent educational professionals and was chartered in 1976. It sponsors professional training institutes, workshops, and conferences; publishes a consultant directory; and offers information about school selection issues to students and their families. Other benefits include member brochures and fliers; the online IECA Information Service Bulletin; webinars; college tours; College Coaches Online, a searchable database for student athlete recruiting; discounts on business services like IECA's professional liability insurance coverage at group rates; shipping services; credit card processing, and customizable forms. There are two membership categories: *professional,* for those with a minimum of three years' experience who have demonstrated a professional mastery of the field; and *associate,* for consultants who are newer to the field. Qualifications for professional membership include a master's degree from an accredited institution (or significant professional experience), professional references, evidence of visits to 50 colleges or universities and three years of experience in counseling or admissions, as well as a minimum number of students advised while employed or working in a private practice. The annual associate-level membership fee is $300; professional members pay $600 a year. Its website is www.iecaonline.com.

- *National Association for College Admission Counseling (NACAC).* This worldwide organization of more than 12,000 members was founded in 1937 to assist students making choices about postsecondary education opportunities. Its members include counseling and admissions professionals.

Annual membership is $215 for educational consultants and includes subscriptions to the quarterly *Journal of College Admission* and the *NACAC*

▲

Express Education

You don't have to commit yourself to another educational degree or certification to get the 411 that can help you be a better educational consultant. IECA offers training programs that are worth exploring. The organization's annual four-day Summer Training Institute for Independent Educational Consulting helps newer consultants learn more about working effectively with students and families, building a knowledge bank concerning the options available to students, managing and promoting the business, and more. The nonmember fee is $1,450, while IECA members in good standing pay $1,275. Educational consultants Steven Antonoff of Denver and Charlotte Klaar of Brunswick, Maryland, have both donated their time to teach in this program.

The organization also offers a full-day training program called "Transitioning to Private Practice College Consulting" specifically for school-based college counselors and university-based admissions counselors who are ready to make the leap to a new career. Refer to the Appendix for IECA contact details if you're interested in attending.

Bulletin, an online newsletter; a national conference, seminars and webinars; a career center, and more. Homebased independent counselors and educational consultants who have three years of college admissions counseling in a secondary school or university setting, or who have a bachelor's degree and three years' experience as an educational consultant or counselor, are eligible to join, so obviously you won't be ready for this one right away. But NACAC's website at www. nacacnet.org is full of useful information in the meantime.

- *National Association of Student Financial Aid Administrators (NASFAA).* If it's your intention to offer financial aid services, you may wish to belong to this organization, which supports

Stat Fact

Mark Sklarow, executive director of IECA, says membership in the organization has more than doubled over the past 10 years. Association projections indicate that those numbers will easily double again very quickly, showing that educational consulting is both a thriving and viable occupation.

student financial assistance professionals at institutions of higher learning. Many of its members are CPAs or certified financial planners, but it also welcomes financial aid administrators such as consultants. Individuals may join as an affiliate member; dues are $770 annually. See www.nasfaa.org.

Industry Publications

There's a veritable cornucopia of publications on the market with content related to college admissions and financial aid issues, but only a handful are written for educational consulting professionals. Here's a roundup of some you may find interesting.

Periodicals

- *ADDitude*: a magazine with information and inspiration for adults and children with attention deficit disorder. Published since 1999; a one-year, four-issue print/digital subscription is $24.99. Subscribe at www.additudemag.com.
- *The Chronicle of Higher Education.* The self-proclaimed No. 1 source of news, information, and jobs for college and university faculty members and administrators has an awesome website at http://chronicle.com with a plethora of free resources, including e-newsletters. Its publication, *The Chronicle*, features subscriber-only content and insight into the issues that matter to higher education professionals. Published weekly by The Chronicle of Higher Education, it costs $82.50 for the print edition, $10 less for digital. Check it out further on Facebook at http://www.facebook.com/chronicle.of.higher.education.
- *Next STEP magazine.* A teen publication distributed in more than 20,500 high schools in all 50 states. It covers college and career planning and life skills, and is a good way to keep up with what's important to today's teens. There's also a free e-newsletter with information about schools, scholarships, and more. It costs $17.95 for a one-year subscription (five issues). Published by Next STEP Publishing. Sign up at http://local.nextstepu.com.
- *U. magazine.* An interesting and fun lifestyle and entertainment publication, distributed at college campuses nationwide, that contains articles about issues that are important to college students. In addition to celebrity interviews, recent issues had stories on avoiding the "Freshman 15," turning an internship into a job, digital plagiarism, the traits of great leaders, and the meaning of dreams. Both the paper and online editions are free. Unless you're regularly on

▲

campus and can grab a copy, sign up for the electronic edition at www.colleges.com/Umagazine (and don't forget to check out its Facebook page).

- *UB University Business magazine*: Although this publication is written for presidents and other senior officers at two- and four-year colleges and universities throughout the United States, *University Business* magazine can provide helpful insight on current and emerging trends in all areas of university and college management. Published monthly in both print and digital form by Professional Media Group LLC, it reports regularly on admissions and financial aid topics. Subscriptions are available at no cost to qualified administrators at colleges and universities, but unless you're still employed as a university admissions counselor, go to www.universitybusiness.com, where you can read past issues at no cost. You'll also find a dozen different e-newsletters at www.universitybusiness.com/user/register that you can subscribe to at no cost.

Books

There have probably been thousands of books published about the college admissions and financial aid processes in the past few decades. Here's a sampling of recently published books for your edification:

- *The Best 377 Colleges* (Princeton Review)
- *The College Finder: Choose the School That's Right for You!* (Wintergreen Orchard House) by Steven Antonoff, Ph.D. (who was interviewed for the book you're currently holding)
- *College Match: A Blueprint for Choosing the Best School for You* (Octameron Associates) by Steven Antonoff, Ph.D.
- *College Unranked: Ending the College Admissions Frenzy* (Harvard University Press), edited by Lloyd Thacker
- *The Everything Paying for College Book: Grants, Loans, Scholarships and Financial Aid—All You Need to Fund Higher Education* (Adams Media) by Nathan Brown and Sheryle A. Proper
- *On the Road: Saving/Paying for College* (Kaplan Business) by Sheryl Garrett
- *Academic Transformation: The Road to College Success* (Prentice Hall) by

> **Bright Idea**
> If your professional interests include working with students who have learning disabilities, the *Journal of Learning Disabilities* is must reading. Published by SAGE Publications, this bimonthly covers topics relevant to the field of learning disabilities. Content includes intervention articles, literature reviews, and research reports. A print/email subscription costs $79.

De Sellers, Ph.D., Carol W. Dochen, Ph.D., and Russ Hodges, Ph.D.

- *Making It into a Top College* (Collins Reference) by Howard Greene
- *Paying for College Without Going Broke* (Princeton Review) by Kalman Chany
- *The Truth About Getting In: A Top College Advisor Tells You Everything You Need to Know* (Hyperion) by Katherine Cohen, Ph.D.
- *Conquering the College Admission Essay in Ten Steps* (Ten Speed Press) by Alan Gelb

> **Dollar Stretcher**
>
> You can get plenty of free insight into and learn a lot about your competition by becoming their follower on Twitter. If you're concerned about looking like a stalker, create a private Twitter list, which is visible only to you, and follow your competitors that way.

Web Resources

If you prefer to surf, you can find a number of educational resources in cyberspace, including:

- *Admissionsboards.com.* This has an admissions bulletin board that's mainly used by people looking for free advice, but it can be interesting to see what they're telling parents and other interested parties.
- *College Goal Sunday.* This national program is held every February in 39 states and Puerto Rico to provide college-bound students and their parents with on-site assistance with filling out the FAFSA, give leads to financial aid professionals, and otherwise help students through the financial aid process. It's the type of worthwhile resource to which you can refer your students and parents. Found at www.collegegoal-sundayusa.org.
- *Free Application for Federal Student Aid.* The online link to the FAFSA is found at www.fafsa.ed.gov.
- *IECA News and Trends in Educational Consulting.* A resource with articles on educational consulting directed toward both parents and educational consultants. Access it at http://development.iecaonline.com/news.html.

> **Smart Tip** *Tip...*
>
> The NACAC conducts a "Space Availability Survey" annually in the spring to determine where openings for qualified students still exist in the upcoming fall freshman class at various colleges and universities. It's a good place to start your student/college match process for latecomers. It can be found at www.nacacnet.org.

▲

- *National Association of Student Financial Aid Administrators (NASFAA)*: This organization has an extensive amount of financial aid information that's worth a look on its website at www.nasfaa.org.

- *Savingforcollege.com*: This site offers information about Section 529 qualified tuition programs. It also has a message board, a scholarship comparison tool, college cost calculators, and information about Coverdell education savings accounts (ESA).

Education

If you're like the educational consultants interviewed for this book, you may already have more than enough education to keep up with the rigors of educational consulting. But if you happen to be interested in the business of consulting, there are a few places you can learn the craft and earn related degrees.

SCORE Some Help

If you're like many small-business owners, you probably know your business specialty inside and out, but you may lack day-to-day business operations skills. Never fear—help is near from SCORE, a nationwide network of retired and working volunteers, entrepreneurs, and corporate managers/executives. This resource partner of the SBA assists hundreds of thousands of businesses reach and then exceed their potential through face-to-face counseling at its 364 chapter offices, email counseling, and inexpensive or free business workshops (both onsite and online). After the onsite workshops, you're always welcome to approach the SCORE counselor and ask specific questions related to your field. Other valuable resources on the website include a wide variety of templates and tools, including a business plan and financial statement template, and much more.

This is truly an awesome resource—and virtually everything is free. Visit the website at www.score.org, or to contact SCORE by phone, call (800) 634-0245.

Academic Programs

The UCLA Extension offers one of the only college counseling certification programs in the country. You must already hold a bachelor's degree to be admitted to the online program, which consists of six required courses and a six-unit practicum.

The following institutions offer counseling degrees, programs, or courses:

- Auburn University: M.Ed. in school counseling
- California Polytechnic State University, San Luis Obispo: M.A. in education with a counseling and guidance specialization
- Central Michigan University: M.A. in counseling
- College Board: counselor workshops
- Elmhurst College Academy for College Admission Counselors: College Counseling 101, 201, and 301
- Iowa State University: M.A. in school counseling
- Marquette University: M.A. in counseling
- National Association for College Admission Counseling: professional development workshops and webinars
- St. Cloud State University: M.S. in college counseling
- University of Massachusetts Amherst: Master's degree in school counseling
- University of Wisconsin Oshkosh: M.S.Ed. in school counseling and student affairs/college counseling

You can find a comprehensive list of school counseling degree programs at the American School Counselor Association website (www.schoolcounselor.org).

For general consulting programs, check out:

- The University of Iowa, Tippie School of Management: MBA with a concentration in strategic business consulting
- Wake Forest University, Babcock Graduate School of Management: MBA with a concentration in consulting

Are you exceptionally skilled at matching students to colleges, but lack financial management skills? Or did you follow a liberal arts curriculum in college and gleefully managed to elude the accounting classes? Then you might want to brush up on the business management skills that can make you a savvier business owner. Local community colleges often offer business management courses like accounting, financial management, and even business law through their continuing education programs, and it's usually unnecessary to enroll in a degree program to sign up. Likewise, adult education programs can be a good place to acquire business skills, particularly if the courses are taught by experienced practitioners.

Finally, the SBA (www.sba.gov) and SCORE (www.score.org—see sidebar on page 86) offer free education, including professional business counseling, through offices nationwide.

Certification

Certification is an excellent way to demonstrate an advanced knowledge of your industry, which in turn inspires your clients' confidence in you. The American Institute for Certified Educational Planners offers professional certification for educational consultants who hold at least a master's degree in a relevant educational field, can submit five professional references, and demonstrate high ethical standards. Applicants must also take a written examination. Recertification is required every five years and is awarded based on sustained professional activities. The certification fee is $400, and there is an annual fee of $75 to keep the certification current. You are entitled to use the initials CEP, for Certified Educational Planner, upon completion of the program.

Conferences

- *IECA spring and fall conferences*. Held in two different locations semiannually, these conferences are attended by independent educational consultants, admissions officers, and administrators from across the country. The conferences feature dozens of workshops, daily networking opportunities, member roundtables, and more. For more information, email info@IECAonline.com.

- *HECA Tour and Conference*. The annual conference provides lectures, workshops and other educational opportunities to HECA members. Networking opportunities, social events, and guided tours of local college campuses are also on the docket. Visit www.hecaonline.org for more information and conference pricing.

Tip...

Smart Tip

Want a quick look at a college from the comfort of your office? Then go to www.campustours.com for a virtual tour. The site also gives useful information such as enrollment statistics, tuition, degrees offered, and sports for thousands of U.S. colleges and universities.

- *NASFAA National Conference.* Held annually in July for financial aid professionals, this conference will probably give you more information than you really wanted to know if you're like many educational consultants who do just general financial aid advising. Still, if you'd like to share war stories about financial aid consulting, this one could be for you. Check out www. nasfaa.org, and click "Events Calendar" for more information.

College Tours

- *HECA Tour and Conference.* As mentioned in the previous section, HECA members who attend the organization's annual conference are invited to take a pre- or post-conference guided bus tour of college campuses near the conference site. It's an easy way to knock off some of the colleges on your list to visit. Look for information at www.hecaonline.com.

- *IECA Members-Only College Tour.* This preconference activity takes member consultants to several colleges over two to three days, depending on the location. More information can be found on the www.iecaonline.org website under "Members," then "Campus Tours."

> **Tip...**
>
> **Smart Tip**
>
> The number of educational consultants who would like to go on consortium tours often exceeds the number of available spots. So organizers will choose from among the applicants who appear to be the best match for the tour. To increase your chances of being chosen, join the Independent Educational Consultants Association and get as much education and experience as you can.

Consortium Tours

Over the past few years, colleges have become very aware that educational consultants "are not the evil people they once thought us to be," says Brunswick, Maryland, consultant Charlotte Klaar with a laugh. "They didn't used to want us to visit because school-based counselors complained about it. Basically their argument was, 'Why should people pay for something they can get for free from school-based counselors?' But today, colleges recognize that educational counselors must be good or they'd be out of business, so we're getting invited to their campuses."

With the exception of the cost of travel to the tour starting point, consortium tours often are all-expenses paid and visit up to a dozen or more colleges in a specific geographic area. On occasion, however, the host schools will contribute a fixed amount for transportation to the host locale, depending on how remote the tour is. Klaar says the stigma once attached to educational consultants has faded so much that there are now college tours specifically for these professionals. You'll find a list of consortia that offer tours at www.nhheaf.org.

Consortia are sometimes more interested in wining and dining experienced educational consultants; therefore, perhaps the best way to see the USA on a tour is to join an organization like IECA, which offers a minimum of three tours a year—including one each before the fall and spring conferences. IECA also sometimes organizes stand-alone tours over three days that might visit 15 or more colleges. Finally, IECA publishes a members-only online College and School Tour Guide with contact names, phone numbers, and email addresses. So overall, it should be pretty obvious that one of the first things you should do when you launch your business is to join a professional organization like IECA. The benefits really are worth the cost of membership.

Strike Up the Band

Now that you've laid the groundwork for your new college admissions and financial aid consulting practice, you're about to take a giant leap forward in its development. You're about to become an advertiser.

If you're the type of person who mutes the sound during TV commercials or fast-forwards through the sales pitches on recorded programs, this may not sound like a good idea to you. After all, it's your reputation and knowledge that will bring students and parents flocking to your door, not a magazine ad or a TV commercial, right?

Well, yes and no. While your reputation definitely will grow as you counsel more and more students, getting them in the door in the first place when you're still relatively unknown takes a little work. So unless you have a ready-made clientele (i.e., you've been counseling for years in a community where everyone knows you), you'll need to implement a targeted advertising strategy that will spread the word that you've hung out your shingle. This chapter discusses the techniques that work best for educational consultants and offers some suggestions on other strategies you can try if you're so inclined.

Your Plan of Attack

Before you ever shell out a single Jackson or any of his higher-value buddies for advertising, you really need to take a step back and draw up a marketing plan. This plan doesn't have to be as extensive or developed as your business plan, but it should include enough detail about the steps you plan to take to attract clients to make it useful. As with your business plan, you should refer to your marketing plan regularly to gauge how well your advertising efforts are doing and to determine whether you need to change course to make those ad dollars work harder. Your initial marketing plan should cover at least three years, which you may recall is the length of time IECA executive director Mark Sklarow says it takes most educational consultants to really start making money in this profession.

Fun Fact

No one really knows who invented the SWOT analysis, although marketing pros say it was definitely in use by Harvard Business School academicians during the 1960s. It may be a classic, but it still has great application for your startup business today.

SWOT Analysis

So what goes into a marketing plan? Basically, it should contain a description of your product (which is a service, in your case), a description of your customer, and details about your advertising strategy. You may have already collected some of this information if you completed the tasks suggested in Chapter 3. So it should be easy to plug this data into your marketing plan, then come up with a well-thought-out advertising strategy and budget.

However, there is one more thing you should do that can give you real insight into your market as you build that advertising strategy: You should consider creating a SWOT analysis. A SWOT analysis is a simple business tool that has been taught in business schools since the '80s. It's a tool that's used by everyone from small-business owners to mega corporations to determine their strategic position in their market and the environment in which they are doing business.

SWOT stands for:

- *Strengths* (the things you do well and those that differentiate you from your competition)
- *Weaknesses* (things that could be improved, as well as anything your competition could take advantage of)
- *Opportunities* (trends and other situations from which you can benefit)
- *Threats* (obstacles or problems that could harm your business)

Marketing gurus recommend writing down these characteristics to help you see exactly where your challenges lie. In addition, as with goal-setting, seeing your strengths and weaknesses in black and white makes them seem more real and of immediate concern.

On page 94, there's a SWOT analysis for a hypothetical educational consultant who is setting up a practice in a medium-sized city of about 30,000 people. You'll also find a blank SWOT worksheet on page 95 that you can use to analyze your own business. Once you have the analysis in hand, you can make some decisions about how you'll advertise to play to your strengths and overcome your weaknesses on your way to educational consulting success. And by the way, it can be very helpful and enlightening to create a SWOT analysis for your competitors. Forewarned is forearmed, as the saying goes.

> **Bright Idea**
> Need inspiration for writing your marketing plan? Then check out the SCORE website at www.score.org, where you'll find sample business plans you can adapt for your own use—or use as a starting point for your own plan. You'll find this wealth of knowledge under the "Templates and Tools" link.

On a Budget

So back to the business of advertising. Once you've completed your SWOT analysis and marketing plan, you're ready to make some decisions about your

▲

Sample SWOT Analysis

Strengths

- 15 years' admissions counseling experience at a leading private school

- Good rapport with teens; patient with doting parents

- Good public speaker

Weaknesses

- Last educational consultant in the immediate area had a shady reputation

- Small-business management skills need development

- Can't travel much until the twins graduate from high school next year

Opportunities

- Ratio of high school counselors to kids in the area is 150:1 (they need me!)

- Nearest educational consultant is based 20 miles away

- Numerous upscale subdivisions are located within a 10-mile radius

Threats

- The nearest competitor is well-established and specializes in Ivy League colleges (also my area of interest)

- Many empty-nesters in the immediate area (no kids left to educate!)

- Local economy has been depressed over the past 12 months

advertising strategy and budget. Experts say that businesses should plan to spend 2 to 5 percent of projected gross sales on advertising, even (or make that especially) during the lean early years. So what to do if you don't have much in the way of gross sales? You might have to use your second- or third-year projections to determine your budget. For example, if you use the $15,000 Year 2 projection figure suggested by Sklarow of IECA back in Chapter 1, your advertising budget would be just $300

SWOT Analysis Worksheet

Strengths	Weaknesses
_____	_____
_____	_____
_____	_____
_____	_____
_____	_____
_____	_____

Opportunities	Threats
_____	_____
_____	_____
_____	_____
_____	_____
_____	_____

to $750. If you project gross revenue of $40,000 in Year 3, your ad budget would be $800 to $2,000.

Most educational consultants finance these ad costs out of personal savings, especially considering how very low they are. And speaking of how paltry these figures may seem, you might think it's not possible to get much bang for your buck. Au contraire—it's all in how you spend that buck. So here's a look at some of the techniques that work best for educational consultants—and some that don't.

House Calls

Looking for a way to distribute your brochures and other advertising materials widely but without a lot of cost or effort? Then team up with the real estate agents in your community. They often prepare welcome packets for home-buying clients that contain information on local businesses, including medical centers, dental offices, restaurants, shopping, and—of course—elementary and secondary schools. They may be more than willing to include your material in the packet at little or no cost. "Real estate agents are naturally your buddies," says Mark Sklarow of the Independent Educational Consultants Association. "New families may not have a chance to get to know the local counselor well [before they need help], and you can step right in."

By the same token, you may find that the local Welcome Wagon will allow you to tuck your brochure into their welcome packet, also usually at a very low cost. Look in the Yellow Pages or Google "Welcoming Service for Newcomers" for leads.

Direct Mail

Direct mail (aka direct marketing) is one of the best and most cost-effective advertising tools available to marketers. The problem is coming up with a way to get the recipient to open the envelope or read the message when he or she gets it. (More on that later.) The two kinds of direct-mail pieces that tend to work best for educational consultants are brochures and postcards.

Brochures

Brochures are hands-down the best advertising vehicles you have because they allow you to present a fairly substantial amount of information in a compact package. A brochure can be as simple as a single-fold piece that fits into a standard No. 10 business envelope or as elaborate as an oversized

> **Tip...**
>
> ### Smart Tip
> Although there is no unwritten direct-mail law saying you shouldn't use your own photo in your promotional brochure, it's usually better to leave it out and focus on your qualifications. Your personal appearance really has no bearing on your ability as an educational consultant anyway, so use the space for more useful details, like customer testimonials.

multifold piece with pop-ups and die cuts. The rule of thumb for brochure printing used to be that you'd pay $1 per four-color piece. But today, with instant access to internet printing companies and instant uploading of materials, you'll pay much less. In fact, one printer we found online charges just $148 for 1,000 8.5-by-11-inch glossy brochures, or under 15 cents each, and will even lay out the brochure for an additional nominal charge. (You'll find this company and a few other leads listed in the Appendix.)

Many online printers have brochure templates you can use for free, or if you happen to have design skills, you can lay out your own brochure rather than using the printer's resources. Microsoft Office Professional comes with Publisher, which has quite a number of brochure templates to select from. (Microsoft Word does, too, but it's not as user-friendly.) After you select a layout, it's pretty easy to type in the copy, download and paste photos or other graphics, and output the file to a CD-RW disk or flash drive that can be taken to a print shop or e-mailed to an online printer.

But if design is not your strong suit, you'll probably want to outsource the project, either to a professional freelance designer or to a college student majoring in art. You can find freelance designers listed in the Yellow Pages or at yellowpages.com under "Graphic Designers" or Google the same term and add your ZIP code to find someone local.

If you need a freelance writer to assist with the copywriting, you also can find one at yellowpages.com or in the Yellow Pages under "Writers." The local university should also be able to direct you to a talented advertising or marketing major, as can any professional advertising organizations in your community. Alternatively, you can try posting the details about your job on a website like Freelancer.com, then have your choice of the writers who apply to do your job.

Information that should be in an educational consultant's brochure includes:

- A list of services with descriptions
- A list of the schools where you've made placements (as soon as you have a list to speak of)
- Testimonials from satisfied customers (very important!)
- A description of your credentials
- Full contact info (name, address, phone, fax, website, email/Facebook/Twitter address, etc.)

It's not necessary to publish your prices in your brochure. If you really want to divulge your prices upfront, as some consultants do, you may want to have them printed on a separate piece of paper that can be tucked into the brochure. Otherwise, your brochure will be outdated every time you raise prices. For an example of an effective educational consultant's brochure, turn to pages 98–99.

Sample Brochure

Front Cover

Back Cover

Sample Brochure, continued

Inside Spread

College is a wonderful place where young people can learn, try new things and grow, both personally and academically. But with the many decisions that need to be made—from selecting the right school from among the country's 3,000 colleges to filling out lengthy applications, seeking student aid and juggling the many steps in the admission process—the college entry experience can seem overwhelming.

Wendie Berry Associates can help. We're experts at navigating the maze leading up to admission to an institution of higher learning. In addition to helping you organize the myriad tasks necessary to obtain that coveted admission letter, we'll work with you and your child to make sure the final college choice is one that is best matched to your child's interests and strengths.

Our Services Include:

- Individualized assessment of strengths, talents, interests and goals
- Review of academic records
- Planning for college placement exams
- Guidance on pre-college curriculum/extracurricular activities for maximum academic impact
- Identification of colleges that best suit your child's interests and abilities
- Instruction in interviewing techniques and ways to maximize campus visits
- Review of college essays
- Advice on financial aid and scholarship opportunities
- Other personalized academic support as needed

Successful Placements

Wendie Berry Associates has placed students at the following universities:

- Arizona State University
- Cal Poly Pomona
- Mount St. Mary's College
- Pepperdine University
- San Diego State University
- Stanford University
- Texas A&M University
- University of California Los Angeles
- University of Michigan
- University of Southern California
- University of Washington
- Wayne State University
- Yale University

About Wendie Berry

Wendie Berry, MA, has been directly involved in the college admissions process since 1992. A graduate of California Polytechnic State University, San Luis Obispo, with a Master of Arts in Education and a specialization in Counseling and Guidance, Berry has been a student advisor at both the secondary and collegiate levels, where she counseled hundreds of students. She has visited dozens of university campuses since establishing her college consulting practice in 2001.

Ready to get started? Call today.
It's never too early to make college connections that click!

(555) 555-5555

Postcards

The second type of direct-mail piece that is useful for new educational consultants is the postcard. It's inexpensive to create, produce, and mail, and as with the brochure, you can include a fair amount of info on it—particularly if you go for the larger size, which measures 9 inches wide by 6 inches high and up. The larger size also means your promotional piece will stand out among the recipients' bills, mailing circulars, and junk mail, because advertising postcards usually are smaller (the standard size is 6 inches wide by 4 inches high). Postcards are useful for things like reminding people to call you because time is running out to apply to college, inviting people to attend any public presentations you make (something discussed in Chapter 10), or just generally calling attention to your availability and success rate.

This is one type of promotional piece you can easily design yourself using one of Microsoft Publisher's dozens of postcard templates. But do take the final version to a print shop or email it to one of the online printing companies when you're ready to print. Outputting your own postcards using a laser printer and Avery postcard stock usually doesn't yield the professional image you're after. You'll find some online postcard printing resources listed in the Appendix.

Don't forget that you don't have to develop your own mailing list for your brochures or postcards—you can simply purchase a targeted mailing list for one-time use. (Refer to Chapter 3 for more details on where to find such lists.) You can print the list on labels and affix them yourself to the cards or envelopes, or if you've purchased a really large list, you can send the materials to a lettershop (which you can find via Google or in the Yellow Pages) to handle the job.

Or if the job isn't too large, you can handle it yourself, as Kansas City, Missouri, educational consultant James Heryer does. Every year, he obtains the names of the honor roll and National Honor Society inductees at selected high schools, because he says they're the most motivated students. That usually works out to about 100 of the 500 students in a public school graduating class or the entire graduating class of a private high school (usually around 100 kids).

"I do a mail merge, print out letters, and send them out while I'm watching 'March Madness' on TV," he says. "People sit on them a lot or they get buried, but eventually they'll call when they have a child who's ready for college."

At the time this book went to press, it cost 33 cents per piece to mail a standard-size postcard (maximum size 6 inches wide

Smart Tip

If you don't have time to send out your own marketing materials, consider hiring a lettershop. Lettershops handle a variety of direct-mail services like addressing, collating, printing, and mailing, plus many also arrange list rentals. Smaller shops will handle as few as 500 pieces. Check the Yellow Pages under "Mailing Services" or Google for local leads.

by 4.25 inches high), while oversized postcards (anything larger than standard) cost 46 cents each.

Letters

While the parents of college-bound teens are likely to be your largest target market, Steven Antonoff, the Denver consultant, points out that you should also target professionals like psychologists, pediatricians, and anyone else who works with kids in this age group. "I recommend sending 'update' letters to professionals who are interested in knowing the skinny about what's important to teens," Antonoff says. "These aren't 'I just want to remind you I'm here' letters. Instead, I might tell them about an article I ran across and tell them they might be interested in it, too, because they see a lot of teens. Then at the end of the letter, I remind them about my services. Good consultants need to do this because it gives them visibility."

Burlington, Vermont, educational consultant Sarah Soule uses a similar approach, but with a different audience. "Every fall, I send out a letter to friends and acquaintances who have kids entering their junior year to remind them I'm here," Soule says. "I've been very fortunate that they refer me to other people, so much so that all my clients have come from referrals."

Business Cards

Yes, your business card should be considered as much a promotional piece as anything else you send out. Make sure you always carry a lot of these low-cost sales tools with you, and give them out liberally, including while you're standing in the line at the post office with your postcards, when you're sitting in the stands at your daughter's soccer game—in short, anywhere you meet people and strike up a conversation. You may not get immediate calls from such efforts, but you'll be surprised how many cards find their way into people's day planners, wallets, or address books, where they reside until the recipient (or a friend/associate/family member) needs your services. Custom-printed business cards on laid or linen stock with a logo run only about $32 for 250 cards and usually include color. Any of the office superstores or many of the various online printers can do the job for you fast and professionally.

Website

Though not advertising in the traditional sense, a website is nevertheless an essential tool for spreading the word about your services, even though you may not get a lot of business directly from it.

"You need a website because not having one is likely to lose you clients," says Sklarow. "If you don't have a presence online, you're immediately suspect because people expect you to be there. Basically a website either helps seal the deal or will cost you the deal."

"You don't get much action from a website, but you do get credibility, so I definitely encourage everyone to have a website," Antonoff adds.

Websites are discussed in detail in Chapter 9.

Facebook and Twitter

Like a website, a Facebook page and a Twitter account are an absolute necessity for reaching today's college-bound students—and their parents. Both online tools have become so ubiquitous and commonplace that people may wonder why you're *not* using social media to "telegraph" your message. Facebook is a great tool for connecting with clients—current and potential—but does require a certain amount of maintenance to keep it fresh and useful to "fans." The good news is you can mount your marketing message on Facebook and Twitter at no charge. Both of these useful social media tools are discussed in more detail in Chapter 9.

Counseling the Counselors

Although some high school and college counselors view independent educational consultants as competitors who are trying to horn in on their gig and make money doing something they do for "free," others recognize that consultants are a resource, not a threat. That's why educational consultants like Whitney Laughlin in Santa Fe, New Mexico, suggest "making friends" with local counselors. "Make appointments with counselors, present your credentials, and ask if they [know any] parents who need help with college planning," she suggests. "School counselors can't moonlight and they want someone to help their kids, so if they trust and respect you, they will refer potential customers to you."

"The best way to make an impression is to establish that you have a knowledge base that goes beyond [that of the] school counselor, and emphasize what you offer that's different and differentiates you from others, like the fact that you can meet with clients in the evening or on weekends," adds Sklarow.

Then there are the other educational consultants in your community. "Don't set yourself up in an adversarial position with other consultants," Laughlin says. "You want them to be allies. So if there are other consultants in the same area where you want to set up shop and they have the same credentials as you do, it's probably better to try somewhere else. But if those consultants are not that good, then have at it and compete like hell!"

Word-of-Mouth

Educational consultants and industry experts agree that referrals are the lifeblood of an educational consulting business. That's because while all the other techniques discussed in this chapter will definitely help you land some new clients, referrals will help you net the most business. Worcester, Massachusetts, consultant Joan Bress believes that's because your credibility quotient goes up whenever someone refers you to another person. "If that person trusts the opinion of the person making the recommendation, then you automatically have their trust, too," she says.

▲

Of course, you can't just turn on the referral faucet and wait for the business to flow in. It takes time to build relationships, and of course, those relationships develop through good customer service. "If a family you've worked with is happy with your work, chances are they will be happy to refer you to the next client—and the next," Bress says.

Referrals also come from other professionals, as well as from overworked high school admissions counselors. For example, Soule knows a lot of counselors from her own work as an admissions director, and she keeps in touch with them. As a result, they refer to her all the time. Finally, being involved in a national organization like IECA or NACAC can lead to referrals from other members. The idea is that other consultants will refer to you because you have expertise in or proximity to a particular college or region.

"I get clients from all around the country," says Judge Mason, the Sedona, Arizona, consultant. "Don't be afraid to talk to other consultants and share information."

High School Programs and Playbills

Programs that are either sold or given out at various high school activities can be reasonably good advertising tools, mainly because they go directly to the audience you wish to reach. Programs created for various high school activities like homecoming, theatrical performances, or graduation usually have ads in the back, and they're usually very inexpensive—perhaps $100 or so. Of course, in the case of graduation programs, your ad is not meant to reach the happy graduates or their parents as much as the parents of students who will be graduating next year or the year after that. On the other hand, research shows that 25 percent of college students do not graduate from the college they initially enroll in, so perhaps you might have an audience among the graduates' parents after all.

You usually don't even have to go to any expense to have the ad created. It's possible that either the students in the school's advertising or art classes will do the honors as a work-study project, or the program may be sent out to an outside company for typesetting. In any event, use the space to congratulate the graduates/athletes/thespians and give your name, business name, and phone number. No hard sell is necessary, especially because, as you know from an earlier discussion, it's quite common for people to save educational consultants' business cards and other information "just in case," then to call when "just in case" becomes "soon" or "now."

Heryer recommends advertising in school newspapers, "but only if they're widely read by parents," he says. "A business card ad might be useful and should be fairly cost-effective."

What Doesn't Work

While it's always possible that you could be the exception to the rule and find great success with one of the following advertising vehicles, experienced educational consultants say to avoid:

- *Yellow Pages ads.* Don't waste your money. "I am not a believer in Yellow Pages advertising," Sklarow says flatly. "Use your money elsewhere."

- *Newspaper ads.* People read the sports section to find the scores for their favorite U. The thought of hiring someone with your credentials would probably never even cross their mind, even with an ad staring them in the face. "I've spoken to hundreds of educational consultants, and five have been successful placing big newspaper ads," says Antonoff. "I've tried it myself, and I might as well have thrown the money down the drain."

- *Free community papers.* You get what you pay for in terms of return.

- *City magazines.* They're glossy and upscale, which would reflect nicely on your business, but magazine ads basically have no value for an educational consultant for the same reason newspaper ads don't work. Plus, you have to advertise a bunch of times to build any kind of name recognition, and that's just too expensive for the return you can reasonably expect. The sole exception to this rule would be if the magazine publishes a special college issue. Then it might be worth your while to spring for a one-time ad—if you keep in mind that, as with your brochure, you may not get an immediate return. To find out whether such an issue is planned, call the publication's advertising department.

- *Classified advertising.* Never, never, never. Absolutely, positively valueless. Not the impression you want to make and not the way to reach people looking for admissions counseling.

There are other low-to-no-cost ways to promote your business. We'll get to those in Chapter 10.

Cyber U

Google. Facebook. Twitter. We hear about them every day, and in fact may use them ourselves every day to send updates on our activities to our friends and fans, check what's on at the local movie theater, or search for grocery coupons. But as a fledgling educational consultant, you need to harness the power of the internet immediately as a way of marketing your business.

▲

These days, people expect businesses to be online so they can see what you're about 24/7. They expect you to have a Facebook page that they can "like." And if you're not out there, you could miss an opportunity to land new business—or at least pique the interest of someone looking for college admissions and/or financial aid counseling.

That point was driven home for Joan Bress, the Worcester, Massachusetts, educational consultant, back in the day when the internet was still more of a novelty than a business tool. "When I was visiting one of my adult daughters several years ago, she went online to find some restaurant information," Bress says. "When I asked why she didn't use the phone book, [my daughter] told me, 'If it's not there, I don't care about going.' That was an 'aha' moment for me—I realized there was a whole new generation of people who had a whole new way of finding information, and I knew I needed to be out there, too."

Surfin' USA

Statistics confirm that you need to be out there, as well. The online statistical resource Internet World Statistics reports that more than three-quarters (nearly 79 percent) of Americans are internet users. With all that connectivity (and Americans' proclivity to take advantage of it), it's a good idea to get a business website up and running as soon as possible.

And of course, in addition to providing instant connectivity to potential clients, there's another good reason for launching a website: It gives you a lot of visibility at a very low cost. Web hosting—which we'll discuss in more detail later—starts at as little as $1.99 per month when web hosts offer deals. You can build a simple site with just a page or two or a complex site with multiple pages and links to other websites.

> **Stat Fact**
> A recent Pew Internet and American Life Project report indicates that 93 percent of American teenagers are internet users. Also, 76 percent of all teens are social media users, while 93 percent of teen social media users have a Facebook account. Their Twitter usage is much lower at 12 percent.

Then you can choose to post something as simple as a "service menu" on your website listing your services, or you can publish information about everything from prices to contract details and more, as Sedona, Arizona, educational consultant Judge Mason does (www.judgemason.org). Your own comfort level will dictate how much you'll want to divulge, although Mason believes publishing more rather than less is the best route.

"It's a low-key marketing approach that makes you look honest," he says. "I put my fees on my website so everything is transparent to those who look. As a result, I've never been stiffed by a client—they all pay, probably because they know right upfront what the fees will be."

The consultants interviewed for this book all agree, however, that they don't necessarily get a lot of new business from their websites. (In fact, Santa Fe, New Mexico, educational consultant Whitney Laughlin says only about 10 percent of her leads come from her website.) Rather, their sites are a good resource for prospective clients who want more information before making a decision. "A website is useful so you don't have to spend a lot of time on the phone telling prospects the same information over and over," Laughlin says. "I often tell callers to look at my website, which has my resume, testimonials, and prices, then to call me back."

You may find, as most educational consultants discover, that referrals provide the bulk of your business. Nevertheless, setting up a website should be a priority for your new business. So in this chapter, we'll take a look at the various ways you can harness the power of the internet both to build business and to help you do business better yourself.

Powering Up

Although you're probably eager to claim your own little corner of cyberspace, it's likely that your chances of constructing that first website yourself are statistically less than sinking a hole-in-one on your next trip to Jupiter. So you definitely should get some professional assistance. A good place to start is with your internet service provider (ISP). Many ISPs offer their subscribers a set amount of space—say, 1GB—at no extra charge for use as a personal web page and provide easy-to-follow tutorials for setting it up. That's enough space to accommodate a few pages of text and some photographs so you immediately have an online presence and a URL you can put on your business cards. However, your web page address will be linked to your ISP, as in "www.yourname@ internetprovider.net," which is an instant tip-off—especially to savvy internet users— that you're online on the cheap. It's a good place to start so you get online immediately, but you definitely should use some of your

> ## Bright Idea
> Want to attract the attention of surfers who are using a browser to find college information? Then try buying search engine keywords, those clickable advertising links that appear on search engine pages. You pay a fee for every hit, and the hope is that these click-throughs will result in new business. One pay-per-click advertiser to try is Google AdWords (http://adwords. google.com).

▲

Keep It Up

One additional benefit of using an established computer designer/consultant to create your new website is that he or she is also likely to offer maintenance services, including website updates and additions. That's a service you'll definitely want to take advantage of, even though it's possible to have your website designed so it's easy for even the most cyber-challenged college consultant to handle those tasks.

But let's face it: You'll probably want to spend your time consulting rather than tinkering with your site. That goes double for doing regular maintenance like system checks, software installation, and other upgrades, even if you don't consider yourself a "computer Neanderthal," like Santa Fe, New Mexico, consultant Whitney Laughlin claims to be. Paying a computer specialist by the hour or purchasing a service contract and allowing an expert to do the work for you are usually better choices.

hard-earned startup dollars to build and launch a custom-designed website as soon as possible.

If you don't have the computer gene in your DNA, don't despair. There are plenty of affordable freelance web page developers around who can help you construct a professional web page. All you do is give them the copy for the site, and they'll create a usable and attractive website using HTML language that can be navigated easily and will have the appropriate links to lead viewers from one screen to the next. For this expertise, you'll pay anywhere from $1,000 to $4,000, a cost that's dictated by the designer's experience, the number of pages on the site, and the complexity of those pages.

To find a computer consultant/web page designer, do a Google search, check the Yellow Pages, log into yellowpages.com, or contact a business organization like your chamber of commerce. If you're really operating on a shoestring budget, try calling the information technology (IT) department of your local university and ask for a lead to a gifted IT major. A student is likely to charge far less than an established professional and also may have an especially fresh and creative approach to the design process.

Another way to get a professional website design is to use one of the templates provided for free by the major web hosts. At GoDaddy.com, for example, you can select from more than 300 templates with 2,000 design options. Or to make the process even easier, you can use one of GoDaddy's 70 prebuilt websites, which literally can get you online in minutes.

The downside to using a prebuilt site is that many, many other people have used the same templates for their butcher shops, tattoo parlors, heavy metal bands ("Demon Breath"), and other businesses—not to mention for personal sites touting everything from Lego castles to "Girls Gone Wild" photos. Still, if your written copy rocks the site, then using a predesigned website won't be that big a deal, at least until you can afford to get a custom-designed site.

On the other hand, if you feel comfortable around CPUs and HTML and have the time to spare, there's no reason why you can't do the design yourself. There are a number of good software packages on the market that will guide you through the process. A couple to look into include Dreamweaver CS6 by Adobe (retails for $399, available at Amazon.com or office superstores) or Microsoft Expression Studio 4 Web Professional (retails for $150 or less, available from Amazon, and computer and office superstores).

Cyber Content

Of course, it's not enough to have a good-looking website; you also need compelling copy that grabs your readers' attention and answers as many of their questions as possible. If you have a knack for writing promotional copy (which is basically what a website needs), you certainly can write the copy yourself. Otherwise, you may wish to hire a freelance writer to assist you. As with web designers, you can find a freelance writer online through organizations like MediaBistro.com and Freelance.com (where you can post details about your needs), and through the Yellow Pages, yellowpages.com, business associations, and university English and communications departments. Depending on the writer's experience, you may pay $500 to $2,500 for website copy.

Some of the useful elements of an educational consulting website include:

- *List of services.* Clearly, this is the most important element on your website, so be sure to include sufficient details here. To begin with, be specific about the scope of the services you offer. For instance, if your main purpose is

Bright Idea

It's usually best to keep the design of your web pages simple. In addition to making it easier for readers to find the information they're after, simply designed pages load faster, which means there's a smaller chance the surfer will move on to another site because yours is taking too long to load.

to offer college admissions consulting, play that information up. Information about lesser services, like, say, financial aid advice, should be given less space and briefer explanations.

- *Your credentials/resume.* This would have to be the second most important element on your website, and the one that will give you the most credibility. It's usually a good idea to publish your entire *curriculum vitae*, with details like educational and academic background, teaching and research experience, publications, presentations, awards and other details, on your site. The more readers know about you, the more likely they are to trust you and your judgment.

- *List of institutions where you've made successful placements.* This gives the reader an idea of the types of colleges/universities you've worked with. Even if the one he or she is interested in isn't on the list, that person will get a general idea of the knowledge you have about various institutions.

- *Workshops and public speaking engagement information.* These face-to-face encounters give prospects an opportunity to see you in action before writing a check for consulting services.

- *Customer testimonials.* These are probably the most powerful sales tools at your disposal—and you don't have to pay a dime for them. Every time you get a letter or email from a satisfied customer, post it on your site—but only after you've obtained written permission from the writer. "People write me notes all the time, although some ask me not to use their names on the website," says Sarah Soule. "Some of them are embarrassed to admit they used a consultant because they think it may look like they're getting an extra edge or maybe because they see us as outside counsel the same way they see someone who goes to a therapist. But everyone needs some help once in a while—there's nothing to be embarrassed about."

  Even so, make sure you respect the client's wishes when you post those testimonials, or else the kind of publicity you'll get as a result could be negative—or worse. (In our litigious society, people have sued for less.)

- *Resources.* Consultants like Joan Bress and Charlotte Klaar include links on their web pages to resources of interest to college-bound students (and tuition-paying parents)—a convenience their clients appreciate. Their websites contain a truly awesome list of links to testing and test-prep sites; scholarship and financial aid sites; websites of interest to actors, dancers, filmmakers, and other creative people; college search sites; online applications, and much more. Far from giving away the store, providing such information makes you look on top of your game, which will certainly appeal to someone in the market for an educational consultant.

Logo Motive

While your designer is busy creating a website for you, you may wish to ask whether he or she can create a logotype, or logo, for your business at the same time. (If the person is more techie than artsy, you may need to hire a graphic artist instead, as discussed in Chapter 8.) As you know, a logo is a visual symbol that represents your company and provides instant name recognition, like McDonald's golden arches or Microsoft's multicolored flying window.

Of course, an academic logo is likely to be a little less flamboyant, but you can still do something creative to give your printed materials real flair. "My logo, which a friend of mine and I developed, gets lots of attention," says James Heryer, the Kansas City, Missouri, educational consultant. "It's very eye-catching, with an admission office building in the background overlaid with the business name."

- *Fee schedule.* If you're so inclined, do include one. Some consultants like Judge Mason like the idea; others would prefer that prospects call for rate information. It's your call.

- *General information articles about the college admissions process.* Providing this information won't give away any of your trade secrets. Rather, it is food for thought for your readers and may help them formulate the right questions and do the correct thinking about the admissions process.

- *Contact information.* If you work out of your home, it's not necessary to give your physical address. Rather, you can indicate where you are located (either by city name or by something more generic like "metropolitan Baltimore area"). But your phone number(s) and email address are a must. You may even want to create a fill-in-the-blank form that the reader can email right back to you with the click of the

Smart Tip

Tip...

For easy readability, always use dark type against a light background on web pages. Some web designers like to be creative and use light type against a dark background, but the result can be harder to read. The same thing goes for busy backgrounds—the type will fight with the design, and the design will win every time.

mouse. It's also a wise idea to include your contact information at the bottom of every linked page of information so the reader never has to look far to find it.

Copy for each of these sections should be kept as brief as possible—preferably, it should be no more than a screen long, because surveys show that cyber surfers get impatient when they have to scroll down as they read and may actually leave your site.

(This is especially important in this age of smartphones and their four-inch screens.) If you have a lot of copy, consider linking blocks of information instead so they pop up on separate pages that fit on a single screen.

Finally, a word about Flash, which is the technology that allows web designers to add animation or interactive elements to web pages. Some companies—including serious ones with high profiles—use Flash intros as a way to grab surfers' attention. The trouble is, Flash intros often take too long to load and play too long for most people's tastes. In addition, people who are returning to the same website more than once may become impatient with the Flash intro. If you really want to have a spinning logo or some other Flash element, make sure your web designer incorporates a "skip intro" button on the page so impatient readers can click their way past it and proceed to the more useful info on the next linked page.

Important note: A casual search of the internet didn't uncover a single educational consultant website with a Flash intro, which might be a good reason for you to avoid Flash, too.

Host Committee

Once you have a fully functional website ready to orbit cyberspace, you need to find a place to launch it, then keep it on course. Web hosts were created just for that purpose. There are probably a million host sites around these days, and they're engaged in a fierce battle to get your business. Web hosting can cost as little as $1.99 a month when there's a promotion, but hosting in the range of $3.50 to $6 is actually more common. Shop around for the best deal, though, because new promotions pop up all the time. Right now, for instance, GoDaddy.com is offering 10 GB of disk space, unlimited transfer, Google Webmaster Tools, and more for just $4.24 a month. On the other hand, the highly rated iPage gives users unlimited disk space and email addresses, and a free domain for life for $3.29 a month. It even offers a free online store for selling books or other materials you may wish to offer.

No matter which company you select, make sure to check its reputation before signing on—and check to see if it offers customer support. We've listed some well-known and highly rated hosts in the Appendix for you to check out.

There's one more thing you have to do before your site is fully operational. You need to select and register a domain name. The domain name is your virtual address in cyberspace, and as such, must be unique. As with web hosting, there are tons of online companies with which you can register that name, and in fact, most web hosts will help you with that task. The fee is usually about $10 per year for a .com domain from a domain provider like Domain.com, which can instantly tell you whether your chosen domain name is unique. But like web hosting, domain registration is very competitive (for example, GoDaddy.com has been known to offer domain registration for as little as $1.99 per year), so it pays to shop around, including informally polling your professional colleagues to find out which companies they've been satisfied with.

Font of Wisdom

No discussion of the internet would be complete without stressing how invaluable it can be as a source of information whether you're wearing your educational consultant or small-business-owner hat. Among the most useful sites for college consultants are the SBA's at www.sba.gov, where you'll find information like business management tips and financing options; SCORE (www.SCORE.org), which is a small-business-mentoring site with connections to local SCORE offices that provides no-cost advice; the National Association for the Self-Employed (www.nase.org), which offers advice as well as discounts on insurance and more; and, of course, *Entrepreneur* magazine's site at www.entrepreneur.com, which also provides valuable information about how to run a small business.

Blogs

A blog can be a great way to connect with both prospective and current student clients and their tuition-paying parents. As you no doubt know, a blog is a short, frequently-updated online journal. As a college consulting professional, your objective for writing a blog will be to position yourself as a voice of authority and dispenser of expert advice when it comes to all things collegiate. You'll do this by posting insight and useful pieces of information that will help college-bound students understand the admission process and help them maximize their chances of being accepted into the college of their dreams.

Blog entries can consist of original content written by you, commentary on pertinent current events, or information posted by others, or even links to information relevant to the college experience. For example, on his blog, Denver consultant Steven Antonoff has a link to a *New York Times* article on the art of studying.

You don't have to be a great writer to blog, but you do have to be committed to posting regularly to keep the content fresh and interesting. To determine whether or not a blog is for you, try writing a series of 10 to 15 sample posts of varying lengths (say, 250 to 500 words each). This will give you a good idea of whether you'll be able to come up with enough new ideas to keep a blog going, as well as how much time it might take out of your busy schedule to keep it updated and viable. If you don't think you can commit enough time to updating a blog personally, consider hiring a content writer to do the job for you.

Blogs can reside on your business website, on a dedicated fee-based blogging platform like WordPress.org, or on a free blogging service (like Blogger.com). However, unless you just want to test the waters to see whether blogging is for you, it's best to avoid the free blogging services, because they tend to be loaded with pop-up ads and may require some level of technical ability on your part to make them work well.

The various blogging platform services usually have easy-to-use templates and useful advice for setting up a blog. If you're technology-challenged or simply too busy to do the due diligence yourself, ask your computer consultant for assistance. You also can find a list of suggested blogging platform services in the Appendix that you can investigate.

Social Networking and Other Internet Tools

Try using a mixture of the following free viral marketing tools—or better yet, use all of them, time permitting—to reach today's tech-savvy, college-bound young people and their parents and/or guardians:

- *Facebook (www.facebook.com)*. There are more than a billion reasons to use Facebook to promote your business: namely, its 1 billion+ active users world-wide. Its chief benefit is as a source of free word-of-mouth advertising: Your Facebook "friends" recommend you to their friends, who recommend you to their friends, and so on. You also can connect and open a dialogue with new prospects, current clients, and other interested parties (i.e., those aforementioned parents and guardians) through your business page.

Basically, a Facebook business page is about relationship-building and brand recognition. Start with a free page to see how well it works for you. Eventually, you may want to add paid "Facebook Social Ads" to your page, which allows you to target your advertising efforts very precisely for the best return on investment.

Jason Brown, a Michigan public relations consultant, says that a Facebook profile allows you to get your brand out to a wide audience base in a short time. "In terms of size, Facebook is the seventh largest country in the world," he says. "That should hit home for any business owner who wants to spread the word about his or her company, its goals, and its objectives really fast."

- *Google+ (www.google.com/+/learnmore/)*. Started in 2011 as a way for people to connect with friends and family in "circles," Google+ is also used to connect with celebrities and other notable people rather like Twitter allows a person to follow (or be followed). You simply set up a circle, admit only those people you want to access it, and post information and pictures at will. This can be an easy way to share information with your current crop of students, clients, and their parents that you wouldn't want to publish for all to see until they sign a contract with you.

- *Twitter (www.twitter.com)*. This micro-blogging tool is a great way to send brief updates about your business or general college 411 to interested parties who choose to follow you. For example, you could remind followers that a deadline for submitting college applications is fast approaching, or you could point them (via URL) to an article in a major publication that discusses job opportunities for graduates in certain academic fields. As with a blog, tweets should be relevant and timely. And don't forget to invite your followers to "retweet" your message, as this increases your reach and word-of-mouth advertising possibilities.

- *LinkedIn (www.linkedin.com)*. You won't land any new business directly using LinkedIn, but you *will* accumulate new contacts, which is just as valuable to a small-business owner like you.

Here's how it works. LinkedIn has 175 million members worldwide, who connect with business professionals through references from their own network of trusted business contacts. So let's say that your banker, with whom you've connected on LinkedIn, knows an architect whose son is desperate to get into Yale. She can introduce you to the architect, who ultimately may introduce you to others in *his* network, and so on.

Start with a free LinkedIn membership to get the lay of the land. Eventually, you may want to sign up for a business membership at $24.95 per month, which opens the door to additional business networking opportunities.

▲

- *YouTube (youtube.com)*. This video-sharing website is not just for posting videos of piano-playing cats or Yeti flash mobs on Mt. Everest. Business professionals are increasingly using YouTube to showcase their products and services, and there's no cost to do so. Simply make a video of up to 15 minutes, upload it to the site, then link it to your website or blog. Subjects to explore in your video can include anything from writing a great college application essay to discussing ways students who are way from home for the first time can get the most out of the college experience. Posting such snippets of advice will help to position you as an expert in your field while putting a face to your name.

- *HootSuite*. Finally, if your head is spinning at the thought of managing all of these social media tools *and* running your consulting business, investigate HootSuite (http://hootsuite.com). This social network management tool helps you to post updates, view site metrics and analytics, and otherwise manage your accounts from a single "dashboard." You can try HootSuite for 30 days for free; thereafter, the cost is $9.95 a month.

Even with the help of a management system like HootSuite, you shouldn't attempt to use too many social media tools when you start out. Brown, the Michigan public relations consultant who is himself a master of social media, recommends staring slow. "Eventually, you do need to have your name out there on as many service networks as possible," he says. "Once you see how they work out, you can pick the two or three that work best for you."

10

Public Dissertations

In a world where a cup of coffee (double mocha latte espresso lite with no foam) costs five bucks, your weekly gasoline bill looks like the national debt, and the finance charges on your credit cards could buy enough hamburgers to feed a small nation, it should come as a very pleasant surprise that you can get free publicity for your educational consulting business if you just know where to look for it. We'd repeat that for emphasis, except that paper is expensive, too. So put your checkbook away—in this chapter we'll show you how to make a big splash with your own public relations program. All it takes is some time and effort on your part—and experienced educational consultants will tell you it's time well spent because the returns for your business can be astronomical.

"Every time I'm quoted in an article [about educational consulting], I get about a dozen calls for counseling," says Kansas City, Missouri, educational consultant James Heryer. "I've signed up clients that way. So the potential to make a lot of money is there just by getting published."

And being quoted in an article or publishing one yourself are just two effective ways to land some free publicity. You also can speak to various audiences about issues of importance to college-bound students, position yourself as an expert, teach a workshop, and network with professionals like admissions counselors, members of organizations like IECA, or participants in a civic group like Rotary International. Here's a look at all of the freebies and how you can grab 'em.

Feature Articles

If you've never had so much as a letter to the editor published, you may think your chances of publishing articles about topics of interest to college-bound students and their parents are remote. Not so. Editors are always eager for articles to fill space, especially when they come in "over the transom" (i.e., unsolicited) and they don't have to pay for them, which is often the case with articles submitted by experts in their field because they're clearly promotional in nature. You don't even have to worry about whether all the semicolons are in the right place or the subordinate clauses are in parallel format—if the basic ideas are good enough, a copy editor will clean up any *faux pas*, slap a headline on the story, and splash it across the "Lifestyles" section or on a website.

Informational articles, how-tos, and checklists are always popular with both magazine and newspaper editors. For instance, a provocative title like "10 Secrets About College Admission" or "How to Write a College Essay They Can't Put Down" will certainly pique the curiosity of an editor—and ultimately, his or her

Bright Idea

Whenever possible, include statistics in your feature articles. Statistics confirm the validity of the data you're presenting and lend credibility to the overall discussion. Start with the internet when you're on the hunt for statistics. The Census Bureau (www.census.gov) is a particularly good source, and the information is free (just cite it properly).

readers. Position the topic negatively and you'll create even more interest, as in "10 Things College Admissions Officers Won't Tell You."

While these types of features are clearly public relations material, editors generally don't take kindly to blatant pitches for business. But they'll usually allow a tagline at the end of a story to the effect of, "Robert Wittman, MA, CEP, is an educational consultant based in Walla Walla. He can be reached at (555) 555-5555."

Now, you may be wondering why in the world you would divulge all your trade secrets, and in print and on the internet, no less, so readers can clip or copy/paste the article and save it forever. After all, you're in this business to earn a living and what you have to sell is information and expertise. But just remember the example of the soccer mom who got her darling boy into the college of his choice and now wants to hang out a shingle. She doesn't have all the knowledge and insight necessary to succeed in this business, and neither will most of the people who read your suggestions for finding the right college and fleetingly think they can go it alone.

"If you give parents the tools to navigate the college admissions process themselves, it usually scares the hell out of them and makes them decide they don't want to do it," says Brunswick, Maryland, educational consultant Charlotte Klaar, who wrote a college admissions column in her local newspaper for seven years. So be sure to include your phone number and website URL at the end of the article so those panicked parents know exactly who to call.

Sharing your knowledge this way in print has yet another important benefit, according to Klaar. "I am perceived as the college expert in the communities where the paper is published," she says. And that, of course, is the enviable position you want to find yourself in, especially when those newspaper clippings or computer screen prints, which are known to lie dormant in a drawer or Day Planner for months or years, abruptly surface when a need for your services arises.

Submitting the Manuscript

Newspaper feature articles usually run about 800 words, while web articles usually are no more than 500 words. Magazines, on the other hand, are usually looking for stories of about 1,000 to 1,500 words. In the case of magazines, your chances of getting published increase if you also can submit

> **Tip...**
>
> **Smart Tip**
> You don't have to write a feature article before pitching it to the media. Instead, just summarize the main points and tell the editor about how many words you'll submit. That way, if the editor isn't interested in the slant, it can be adjusted, or if the idea isn't quite right, it can be abandoned. Either way, you save time.

a sidebar, which is a brief story with extra information that accompanies the main story. Submitting photographs with your article also can significantly increase the chances that it will make it into print or onto a business's website.

A manuscript should be typed as a double-spaced Word document with 1-inch margins, then saved in both .rtf and .doc format. If you'll be emailing the article, which is the form most editors prefer, be sure to attach both document files and paste the article into the body of the email just in case the recipient is cagey about opening attachments.

While it's considered pretty low-tech, it's still acceptable to submit manuscripts on 8.5-by-11 white bond paper with 1-inch margins on all sides, although you also should save the article to a CD and send it along with the paper copy. As a courtesy, enclose a self-addressed stamped envelope with your manuscript so it can be returned to you if the editor is not interested in publishing it, or simply indicate in a cover letter that it's not necessary to return the manuscript to you. No matter how you submit your article, be sure to check the publication's writers' guidelines to find out which form the editor prefers for submissions.

The editor will not be expecting your manuscript, so always send it with a brief pitch letter that explains what the article is about and why it would appeal to the publication's readers. A pitch letter should be no more than a few paragraphs long, or about two-thirds of a page at the most. Calling the newspaper or magazine to find out the name of the editor (or checking the publication's website) is always a good idea, because addressing your letter to an actual person increases the likelihood it will be opened. It's also far more professional and courteous to send it to a real person.

A few days after you email or mail the article, call the editor (or his/her assistant) to ask whether the article was appropriate for the publication's audience. And by the way, don't be discouraged if editors are not initially panting to publish your work. It takes a while to break in, which is why it's a good idea to start at the local level rather than regionally or nationally when you're trying to get stories into print or online. Plus, there's something to be said about sheer persistence: Seeing new articles regularly crossing their desks—either physically or electronically—is usually sufficient enough to get editors to sit up and notice, or at least to wear them down.

Once an article does get into print, make sure to note that fact both in your other promotional materials and on your website. Being a published author on topics relating to your area of expertise cements your reputation as an expert in that field.

And speaking of being an authority, there's another residual benefit to the process of sending articles to editors, even if you never see one get into print. Just sending such

---

Newsworthy Notes

If you don't feel up to the task of writing feature stories—or you simply don't have the time—there's another easy way to get free face time in the press. Try sending out a news release to local media outlets.

As you may know, a news release is like a little ad that focuses on something positive about your business. It could be on a topic like your winning streak of getting every student who applies admitted to the Ivy Leagues, or on a process like how to write a spectacular college essay. In any event, the information should be seen as newsworthy, which means timing is everything (e.g., a story about applying for college shouldn't go out around Christmas, when editors' attention is elsewhere).

News releases should be about one page in length and should include full contact information at the top so editors know who to call for more information or an interview. The release should answer the "Journalism Six"—Who, What, Where, When, Why, and How—and provide enough details to make the story provocative and interesting.

Releases can be sent to print media like newspapers, magazines, and business publications, as well as online publications. But don't forget talk radio stations, cable TV stations, and the local network affiliates. They're always on the lookout for newsworthy information that they can turn into "lifestyle" feature stories. And don't be surprised if you one day receive a call with a request to come right to the studio. Whenever possible, be responsive, and you could become that station's regular educational consulting guru.

stories to the media regularly immediately positions you as an expert. The media are always on the lookout for experts, so it's likely that someone will file away your contact information so an editor can call on you the next time a quote is needed about college admissions, financial aid, or other related topics. And cha-ching—you get more free publicity, and you didn't have to do a thing to make it happen except talk and offer your opinion.

Speak Up and Speak Out

Here's another way to gain visibility for your business that's virtually rejection-proof: Offer to give a talk on college admissions topics. You usually can't miss with this technique because organizations are always searching for speakers for their membership meetings. Seek out those organizations whose members fit the profile of the types of people who use educational consultants. After a presentation, you could find yourself with an onslaught of inquiries about your services, a percentage of which will turn into actual business.

Sarah Soule, the Burlington, Vermont, consultant, discovered this firsthand. Her first client was a person who heard her speak as a participant in a panel discussion at the local high school. "I met her for coffee at Barnes and Noble, and I was on my way," she says. "The client never even balked at my fee, and in fact referred me to another student right away."

Membership groups usually pay a very small honorarium or nothing at all to guest speakers, so don't count on paying any bills with the proceeds. Rather, look ahead—you could snag new business just from talking to the membership groups that regularly use speakers, including:

- Rotary club
- Kiwanis club
- Chamber of commerce
- Soroptimist International
- PTA organizations
- Economic clubs

And don't overlook the less obvious groups. For example, the ladies' hospital auxiliary might be a good place to tell your story if the members are 40 to 45 years old and middle-to-upper income. In truth, just

Bright Idea

Because the SAT and ACT are always changing and evolving, you could find a receptive and eager audience at high schools for a presentation on what's different, how to interpret the results, and what strategies can improve a student's scores. Try emailing or mailing details about what you'll cover to local high school counselors and see what develops.

about any group has possibilities, although as Mark Sklarow, executive director of IECA, says, "Always look at the demographics of the group. Many organizations consist of older white males, and do you need to be talking to 65-year-olds about college? But if you've got a free moment and the chamber of commerce is desperate for a speaker, why wouldn't you do it? You could talk about how grandparents can help their grandchildren succeed."

> ### Bright Idea
>
> Grab some high-visibility publicity by donating a professional service to a fund-raiser event like an auction. You could donate some time to help a student write a polished college essay or to help him or her make college selections. In return you'll get your company name in a pro-gram and maybe even on TV. It's a great investment in your business.

"People come to me to ask me to do presentations all the time," says Worcester, Massachusetts, consultant Joan Bress, who has spoken to groups from as small as a handful of people to as large as several hundred folks. "My reaction always is, 'Give me time to change my shoes, and I'll be there.' Those opportunities are that important."

Teaching a free workshop is another way to gain visibility for your business. Santa Fe, New Mexico, educational consultant Whitney Laughlin has done this successfully at local high schools in the past, and still gives several free workshops every year even though her business is well established. "I do several workshops a year on college admissions and financial aid planning," she says. "It's a great way to establish your credentials with both parents and high school counselors, and it definitely generates leads."

And incidentally, Laughlin says that counselors—high school and college alike—usually will not feel threatened or be upset that you're treading on their turf. "In my experience, they're usually great about [me coming in]. They recognize that after visiting more than 600 college campuses in more than 25 years, I have more experience than many school counselors do, and they value that."

Members Only

If you have any time left after writing all those articles and talking to various organizations, there's still one more way you can build a reputation and drum up new business. You can join one of those organizations yourself. Civic, business, and charitable groups often have meet-and-greet sessions specifically designed to encourage interaction among members. In addition to being a source of new leads, such networking opportunities give you a place to cultivate relationships that can result in business.

In some cases, members may even barter for goods and services, which is something that could work to your advantage. Say you need new stationery and business cards and you happen to strike up a conversation with a printing company owner whose daughter is in the ninth grade. You could trade an hour-long consultation on how to approach the college application process for the printed materials. Best of all, when that child reaches junior high age, that doting father may call you for additional services—no doubt in response to your friendly wave at every membership meeting and the materials you keep sending him after adding his name to your mailing list. The bottom line is: Take advantage of every opportunity that comes your way to promote yourself and you'll find the business will begin to roll in.

Handling Negative Publicity

Before we conclude this discussion of self-promotion, there's one more type of publicity we need to address because it's pretty likely you'll encounter it in some form as you launch your business: That's bad publicity generated by those who get into this profession with the intention of deliberately scamming unsuspecting people. Their *modus operandi* usually includes charging exorbitant rates and making promises they can't keep, which reflects badly on every other honest educational consultant.

If you were a college admissions or other kind of counselor in your past life, you're probably already well aware of this unfortunate situation—as well as the fact that there are many more educational consultants who are honest and have impeccable integrity than there are cheaters. However, it can be difficult to combat this type of publicity, especially when you may be accused of taking money from people who have a great need for financial aid.

One way to head off bad publicity is to do as Sedona, Arizona, consultant Judge Mason does and publish your rates and other pertinent information right on your website. "I take a low-key approach to my whole business," he says. "By putting my fees on my website everything is transparent and honest, and after talking to me for five minutes people know I am open and friendly. As a result I don't get much resistance from people."

Furthermore, Steven Antonoff in Denver recommends staying away from the financial planning side of financial aid, which is the area that is often problematic. "Financial planning is really a separate area," he says. "Although we are sensitive to and knowledgeable about financial matters, what we specialize in is offering a very personal service, and it's best to focus on that. The people who are successful have an ethical base and integrity, and if the customer gets references, learns about the consultant's specialty, and finds out how long [he or she] has been in business, there shouldn't be a problem."

"Seventy-five percent of my clients apply for financial aid," adds Laughlin, who has worked as a financial aid director in the past. "I do financial aid counseling when requested but I refer questions about tax planning, IRS stuff, and other financial matters to a certified financial planner."

Finally, to deal with accusations that you are charging for work that high school counselors do for free as part of their jobs, James Heryer says, "Counselors tend to be territorial, and you have to deal with that delicately and put your job into perspective. From the initial interview, I position myself by saying I'm not a substitute or a replacement for counselors; I'm actually supportive of them. I know they're doing a good job. But I also know they are likely to be counseling 200 to 300 kids, and I can help them by giving students a foundation from which to spring."

Financial Aid

Now that you've studied the full slate of tasks required to launch your own college planning consultant business, you're almost ready to take on the world as a newly minted graduate of Entrepreneurial Success 101. But before you can don your figurative cap and gown, you still have to pass a final exam that covers all the financial matters discussed throughout this book. We call that final exam an income and expenses (I&E) statement, and it's more than just a one-time test. Rather, your I&E will serve as your ongoing financial textbook for keeping your business solvent and strong.

Basically, an I&E is a monthly snapshot of both your accounts receivable and accounts payable. Estimating your expenses this way at the genesis of your business is especially important because it will tell you

Bright Idea

Keep a copy of your I&E statement with your tax return. If the IRS ever wants to have a friendly chat about your business, you'll have all the information and documentation you'll need to go to the meeting with your head held high.

whether your income is likely to cover your expenses, whether there will be any money left to salt away after paying those bills, and whether you need an infusion of cash to keep the business going until your revenue satisfactorily exceeds your expenditures.

And don't be surprised as you work through this chapter to find out that your first-year financials actually will be in the red. As you'll recall from Chapter 1, experienced educational consultants and industry experts alike say that the first year can be pretty lean for a new business owner—if not entirely income-free. But once you pay your dues—i.e., make fact-finding trips to universities and acquire the expertise and knowledge you need to be a valued resource to college-bound kids—your revenue can soar.

To give you the most realistic picture of the typical evolution of an educational consulting business, we have provided sample I&E statements starting on page 141 for your consideration. First are Year 1 statements that show net losses for Wendie Berry Associates, a fictitious sole proprietorship with one employee (the owner) that's based in a home office, and College Bound Consultants, a sole proprietorship with two employees (the owner and a 10-hour-a-month clerical person), and higher business expenses overall. The Year 2 I&E statements show a modest net profit for both businesses, which is what typically happens in the second year of educational consulting businesses. We've also provided blank I&E worksheets on pages 143 and 146 that you can use to estimate your own first- and second-year costs.

Let the exam begin.

Tracking Expenditures

Among the typical expenses incurred by educational consultants are:

Mortgage/Rent

Although we're assuming that your educational consulting business will be homebased, there's always the chance that you'd prefer to establish an outside office where you can meet with clients. The cost of your rent would go in this space.

Phone Charges

As we discussed in Chapter 6, it's imperative to have a dedicated business phone for your new business. To keep the cost down, you'll probably want to have a second residential line installed, which will cost $30 to $40 a month, as opposed to a business line at $150 to $400 a month. If you want to have a dedicated fax line, that will add another $30 to $40 a month to your monthly expenses. In addition, voice mail or an answering machine are also a must.

Telecom companies usually offer cafeteria-style plans where you can pick and choose which services you need. But a bundled service package that includes premium services is usually the most affordable choice. For instance, Sage Telecom has a service plan that includes local service, one hour of long-distance calling, and free call forwarding, caller ID, call waiting, and repeat dialing for about $25 a month, plus taxes. (Voice mail is usually extra on most plans and costs about $5.) Having a cell phone (and who doesn't?) with unlimited service will add another $70 or so to your monthly costs.

> **Dollar Stretcher**
>
> Save a lot on your phone bill by switching to an internet-based VoIP service. Using an adapter, touchtone phone, and high-speed internet connection, you can make unlimited calls worldwide for as little as $25.99 a month. Premium features like voice mail and call waiting are included. A few VoIP providers include Vonage, net2phone, and Skype.

Office Supplies

After your initial investment of about $150 for office supplies in your startup budget, you probably won't need much more than pads, pens, folders, and sticky notes on a regular basis. As a result, it should be safe to assume that $50 will more than cover all your supply needs every month. That buys a lot of paper and pens, so you'll have money left over most months to cover the occasional purchases of toner cartridge at $25 to $80 (and possibly more for laser printer cartridges) and copier paper ($25 to $50 per case). We've used $15 for our low-end I&E and $50 for the higher-end business.

▲

Cost Cutters

In the lean early days of your new business, it's always a good idea to keep costs down wherever possible. One easy place to do this is with your office supply budget. To begin with, you probably have enough pens, pencils, legal pads, and paper clips in your desk right now to launch your business, so a trip to the office supply store (no matter how fun it might be) won't be necessary immediately. But for other items you may need, like presentation folders, paper for your new printer and so on, buy in bulk to increase your savings. Office superstores like OfficeMax and even warehouse stores like Sam's Club offer bulk discounts on many everyday office products. And if you buy at least $50 worth of product online from the office superstores, delivery to your home office is usually free. You can drum up some pretty darn good prices on office supplies through online auction houses like eBay as well. Just be sure to consider the mailing costs before you bid. Items like paper tend to be heavy, and you could see all of your savings wiped out after you pay for shipping and handling.

Postage

While word-of-mouth and referrals are the ways you're likely to get most of your business, you may want to try doing a mailing or two to spread the word about your services. At publication time, the cost of first-class postage is 46 cents per ounce for letters and 33 cents for postcards less than 6 inches wide by 4.25 inches high. Oversized postcards mail at 46 cents each. In addition to figuring in the cost of a mailing, don't forget to include extra money in your budget to cover other business-related mailings you might do, including paying your business bills by mail.

Depending on the amount of mailing you do, $25 to $50 a month should be plenty. ($50 in postage will allow you to mail 108 letters or 151 small postcards.)

Salaries

You're probably not really likely to hire staff when you launch your educational consulting business. However, we've included two lines for wages on the I&E anyway—one for the owner's salary and one for employee wages. Even if you choose to put your salary in the bank because a spouse or significant other is covering your household

Beware!

While the IRS expects new businesses to have losses at first, you still must show a net profit in at least three out of five years to be considered a for-profit business rather than a hobby. So keep meticulous records about your expenses and any losses every year just in case the IRS comes calling.

expenses, or you plow all of it into travel or other expenses, it's really important to include a salary for yourself in your monthly expenses. That's the only way you can prove your income, which will be important when you want to buy a house, finance a vehicle, or apply for credit. That figure on the salary line will give you the paper trail you need to prove your business is viable. And of course, because you are an employee—even if you're the only employee—taking a regular salary helps you visualize exactly how much your company is worth and gives you the appearance of being the legitimate businessperson you are.

Now, you may recall from Chapter 1 that Mark Sklarow, executive director of IECA, says you're likely to earn little or nothing the first year because it takes time to get established. So you'll find a net loss showing up on the first-year sample I&E. But never fear—if you're like many educational consultants, that situation will turn around possibly as soon as your second year, and likely in your third year.

When it comes to employee wages, we will assume that if you do, indeed, hire any helpers, your needs will be minor. As a result, you're likely to pay them by the hour, and of course you probably won't offer them any benefits. Clerical workers or researchers can start at the federal minimum wage, which is currently $7.25 in many states. (Because quite a few states have their own minimum wage laws, check with your state's department of labor for the correct amount.) You'll keep your helper longer if you offer a little more per hour, like $7.50 an hour. We've based the salary figure found on College Bound Consultants' Year 2 I&E on an employee earning $7.50 an hour and working 10 hours a month.

Taxes

If you're an employer, you have to withhold taxes on your employees' wages. But here's a news flash: If you pay an employee less than $600 a year, it's not necessary to pay any of the armload of taxes the Fed imposes, or to withhold income taxes from your employee or issue a W-2 or Form 1099-MISC (depending on whether the person is an actual employee or a contract employee). If you were paying $7.50 an hour to a file clerk or a person to answer the phone, for instance, you could get almost 80 hours of work from that person without the nuisance of the federal paperwork. That should be plenty of time to get the jobs done that you're likely to encounter in your first year.

▲

Here's another reason to keep the first-year payroll expenditure down: Your tax liability with an employee will include:

- FICA (aka Social Security tax): 6.2 percent
- Matching portion of Medicare tax: 1.45 percent
- Federal Unemployment Tax: another 6 percent on the first $7,000 paid to an employee, although you may be eligible to claim a 5.4 percent credit if you paid state unemployment insurance (see below)
- State unemployment tax: varies by state
- Workers' compensation insurance: varies by state

Smart Tip

Tip...

For more information about the employee/independent contractor distinction, review IRS Publication 15-A, "Employer's Supplemental Tax Guide," and Publication 1779, "Independent Contractor or Employee." Both are available at no charge at IRS field offices (find one at www.irs.gov), or download them at www.irs.gov.

Assuming you'll be eligible for that 5.4 percent credit, your federal liability alone will be 8.25 percent per employee—plus you still have to worry about state taxes. The bottom line is this is a real buzz kill for a small-business owner. That's why a lot of startup entrepreneurs choose to use contract labor instead, and let them worry about all the taxes.

But beware. Uncle Sam has very strict definitions of what constitutes an employee vs. a contractor based on three factors: behavioral (whether the employer controls how the employee does his or her job); financial (how the individual is paid, whether expenses are reimbursed, and so on); and relationship (whether the employer provides employee-type benefits, and so on). Keeping the wages under $600 will help you avoid any potential tax snafus, but to make sure you're on the right side of the law, you might want to talk to your accountant.

Of course, you'll have to pay taxes on your own earnings. Sole proprietors must pay estimated taxes quarterly on any income earned or anticipated, and because you're new at this consulting thing it can be difficult to estimate your tax liability. Speak to your accountant for guidance. And be prepared for a shock: Homebased businesspeople pay *a lot* of taxes on their wages because they're hit with a self-employment tax (13.3 percent in 2012), which consists of the other half of the Social Security and Medicare taxes that you're now responsible for as the employer of record. The situation is similar for S corporation owners. You'll have to pay estimated taxes on earnings, even if they're all plowed back into the corporation. The top corporate tax rate is currently 35 percent, so be sure to take every legitimate tax deduction to which you are entitled to offset this huge and virtually unavoidable tax bite. One deduction to take, of course, is a deduction for your vehicle expenses. Refer back to Chapter 6 for information on how to maximize your transportation deduction.

Tax issues tend to be fairly complex, especially for a business neophyte whose training and strengths lie in a different direction (i.e., educational consulting). That alone might be a good reason to hire an experienced accountant as discussed in Chapter 5.

> **Smart Tip** _Tip..._
>
> SCORE offers a number of useful business planning tools on its website at www.score. org. Among the offerings, all of which are free: sample business plans and financial statements; a marketing plan budget; and business calculators to help you to calculate startup costs, analyze cash flow, and perform a break-even analysis; and cash-flow projection tools, among other things.

Accounting Services

Speaking of accountants, here's where you'll note their fees. As we mentioned in Chapter 5, a homebased accountant may charge $75 an hour or more, so your task after finding your _numbermeister_ is to figure out how many hours he or she will need to handle your books every month, then do the math to get a figure to plug into your I&E. It's probably reasonable to assume that your accountant won't need more than three to five hours a month to handle your work, which may include tax filings, receivables/payables, and any other financial tasks you'd like to turn over. To find out how much to enter on your I&E, try calling around your community to find out the going rate for accountants, or use the median salary reported for accountants in the _2012-2013 Occupational Outlook Handbook_, which was $61,690 in 2010, or $29.66 an hour based on a 40-hour workweek.

Bookkeepers are more affordable, at $34,030 annually, or $16.36 an hour. We've taken the middle road between that figure and the $75 an hour earned by the self-employed accountant mentioned earlier and plugged $50 into the Year 2 I&E samples to represent one hour of accounting work per month, because your needs will likely be modest until you start making some real money.

Legal Services

As we mentioned in an earlier chapter, once you have developed a contract for clients and filed for incorporation, if you're so inclined, your legal needs will probably be quite modest. For this reason, we have chosen not to include a figure for monthly legal services on our sample I&Es, because we've already included this cost on the startup expenses worksheet in Chapter 6. Depending on your personal situation, you

▲

On The Road Again . . . and Again

During the startup phase of your business, you'll want to keep your expenses as low as possible to keep the drain on your precious startup resources low, too. One way to do this is to monitor your travel costs closely. Try to schedule as many campus visits as possible in the same general geographic area so you can economize on the cost of airfare, transportation, lodging, and other costs.

This is the technique educational consultant Joan Bress uses successfully. Typically she'll visit one to two schools per day during a weeklong trip, plus she'll use every possible opportunity—no matter where she happens to be—to visit campuses. "If I'm somewhere on vacation, my husband knows at some point I'll disappear for three hours and visit the local universities," she says. "It's important to plan your travel time well and take advantage of every opportunity that presents itself to make visits."

may or may not choose to emulate this example. If you find later that you suddenly do need legal representation, it will be an easy task to insert a figure at that time.

Insurance

Using the figures you researched and noted on the insurance worksheet on page 60, divide the total cost of your insurance premiums by 12 and insert that figure on the insurance line of your I&E. We've used a figure of $25 a month ($300 annual premium/12 months) in the sample I&Es.

Online Service Fees

You're probably already paying for internet service to support your Angry Birds habit or to give your kids access to online resources for homework. When you use your online service only for business purposes, it's 100 percent deductible. Typical ISP charges are:

- Standard dial-up ISP: about $9.95 per month
- ISDN ISP: starts at $14.95 a month
- DSL: about $19.95 a month

- Broadband high-speed satellite internet: around $29.95 a month, plus basic cable TV service (at the very least)

You'll also have to pay for web hosting if you have your own website. The cost starts as low as $1.99 for 1 GB of space, which may be enough for your purposes. We've used a figure of $5 a month because it buys you many valuable extra perks, like unlimited disk space and email addresses, and domain registration.

Advertising

This is one area where you may have to bend the rules a little so you can crank up your soon-to-be-moneymaking marketing machine. As mentioned previously, marketers suggest earmarking 2 to 5 percent of your gross revenue for advertising efforts. But because it's quite likely that your first year will be a break-even year at best, the 2 percent rule doesn't apply. So initially, it would be wise to set aside some funds, even if they must come from personal savings or a business loan. Never fear—you'll get the cash back later when your business takes flight. We've used a figure of $50 a month in our low-end sample and $100 on the high end. Obviously, that won't buy much, but it will get you started.

Travel

This stands to be one of the biggest expenses you'll incur when you start your business. Steven Antonoff, the Denver educational consultant, says he spent six months traveling to colleges before he ever saw a single client—and as you can imagine, that can be costly. "The expectation is that you'll spend $5,000 to $10,000 a year on travel costs, but the reality is you can do it on far less," he says. "Of course, if you can afford more, it increases your learning curve. A lot depends on where you are doing business. If you're in New England, the mid-Atlantic area, or California, where there's a concentration of universities, a budget of $1,000 to $2,000 is reasonable. But in the Midwest, $5,000 is a drop in the bucket."

But there are easy ways to keep your costs down, not the least of which is to drive rather than fly to your destinations (at least until gasoline prices take flight again) or to take advantage of airline deals like Antonoff does. In addition, as discussed in Chapter 7, many consortium tours welcome consultants who are members of IECA or the other college admissions associations. The consortia usually cover all expenses except the cost of travel to the startup point, so it's pretty easy to keep a lid on travel costs.

Still, you'll have to expend a certain amount of cash to meet up with consortium tours or to travel on your own. The costs will, of course, depend on the distance you must travel, the mode of transportation (even with higher gas prices it may still be more economical to take a road trip), the caliber of the lodging, and so on. We've estimated high, as Antonoff recommends, and used a figure of $4,800 per year, or $400 a month, on our I&E to represent the cost of expenses like airfare, lodging, and a rental car.

Transportation/Maintenance

This is where you'll note the cost of local transportation, including trips to clients' homes or other meeting spots and treks to the post office to send out advertising materials or pick up mail from your post office box. Mileage, wear and tear on your vehicle, and the cost of gasoline, windshield wiper fluid, regular maintenance like tune-ups and oil changes, and bridge and tunnel tolls are all deductible expenses when they're incurred in the line of duty. In addition, the cost of public transportation like taxis, buses, or the subway to get you to and from a client's home or other business location is also deductible. We have earmarked $100 on our I&E samples; you may find you need more than this after you do some preliminary calculations.

Magazine Subscriptions/Books

Any publication purchased for use in the business (even *Mental Floss*, a publication for "knowledge junkies") is deductible, including publications left out for clients to read while they wait for their appointment. Tally up the subscription prices and divide that cost by 12 to get a figure to insert on this line. You might also include a little extra padding in the cost in case there are business books you'll want to pick up throughout the year.

Membership Dues

As mentioned in a previous chapter, professional organizations are a great place to glean new information, network with peers, and otherwise get tuned in to your new profession. Choose the organization that interests you most and insert one-twelfth of its annual membership cost on this line.

Miscellaneous Expenses

To be prepared for those unexpected expenses that always seem to crop up, be sure to include a little extra scratch in your I&E. An amount equal to 10 percent of your estimated monthly costs should be sufficient.

Tracking Receivables

Back in Chapter 5, we were pretty adamant about the need to hire an accountant or bookkeeper to keep your financial locomotive on the rails. But, of course, it's not necessary to use an accountant for every financial detail—and, in fact, if you do, you'll probably end up counseling the bookkeeper's own offspring because you'll have vicariously paid their tuition single-handedly. Therefore, it's recommended that you keep an eye on your own finances informally using an accounting software package. The leading accounting software is QuickBooks Pro, an easy-to-use program for both single- and double-entry bookkeeping that has core accounting features like invoice creation, sales and expense tracking, business plan creation, time tracking, and more. In addition, you can export data from QuickBooks to TurboTax at tax time, or import information from Excel if you prefer to keep records in that program. QuickBooks Pro retails for about $250 and is sold at office supply and computer stores everywhere. Another accounting package you can check out is Sage 50 Complete Accounting. A single-user copy retails for $369 and is available from computer stores and directly from Sage (http://na.sage.com).

Financing Options

While it's clear from our earlier discussion of home business expenses that the outlay of cash to start a college planning consultant business is usually quite low, you may find that your budget won't stretch quite far enough to cover those travel expenses we mentioned. If that's the case, you may want to secure some financing. Now, we won't kid you: It can be difficult for a fledgling business to obtain startup capital from a traditional lender like a bank. Quite frankly, banks usually prefer to do business with companies that are well established and have a verifiable record of success. You're likely to need only a fairly small loan to cover your travel costs (say, $5,000 for the first year), so you may find it's easier and less labor-intensive to apply for an unsecured loan from your bank or credit union. If the thought of going into debt makes you cringe, you might instead cash in some stocks, bonds, certificates of deposit, or savings bonds to get your startup stake. It's also possible to borrow from retirement funds like pension plans, IRAs, 401(k) plans, SEPs, and Keoghs. If you do end up borrowing money from any source, be sure to include the monthly repayment amount on your I&E statement.

There's one final source of funds you may wish to consider, and it's not a home equity loan, because banks generally make it a practice not to give those out to fund small-business ventures. Rather, Uncle Sam's own Small Business Administration (SBA) offers many programs for startup business owners. Besides loan programs, the SBA offers free counseling and training seminars on topics like marketing plan development. Check out the SBA's deep resources at www.sba.com. You also can call the SBA answer desk at (800) 827-5722 or email answerdesk@sba.gov for assistance.

Adding It Up

If you're like the educational consultants interviewed for this book, your monthly expenses should be fairly modest, which should be a relief considering that your monthly income is likely to be just as modest (if not nonexistent) in the first year. Hopefully, your personal savings or other readily available sources of cash will be able to cover these costs easily, so by the second or third year, when you do start to make some real money, you'll be in the black fairly quickly.

Sample I&E Statement—Year 1

Wendie Berry Associates

Projected monthly income:		$0
Projected monthly expenses:		
Mortgage/rent		
Phone (office and cell)	$40.00	
Postage	$25 .00	
Office supplies	$15.00	
Owner salary	$0	
Employee wages	$0	
Taxes	$0	
Advertising/promotion	$50.00	
Insurance	$ 25.00	
Legal services	$0	
Accounting services	$0	
Travel	$400.00	
Online service	$20.00	
Web hosting	$5.00	
Transportation/maintenance	$100.00	
Subscriptions/dues	$40.00	
Loan repayment (startup expenses)	$ 0	
Miscellaneous (10 percent of total)	$72.00	
Total expenses	**$792 .00**	
Projected income/Expense total		**−$792.00**

▲

College Bound Consultants

Projected monthly income:		**$0**
Projected monthly expenses:		
Mortgage/rent	$ 500.00	
Phone (office and cell)	$170.00	
Postage	$50.00	
Office supplies	$ 15.00	
Owner salary	$ 0	
Employee wages	$75.00	
Taxes	$ 6.25	
Advertising/promotion	$100.00	
Insurance	$ 25.00	
Legal services	$0	
Accounting services	$0	
Travel	$400.00	
Online service	$30.00	
Web hosting	$5.00	
Transportation/maintenance	$100.00	
Subscriptions/dues	$40.00	
Loan repayment (startup expenses)	$200.00	
Miscellaneous (10 percent of total)	$170.00	
Total expenses	**$1886.25**	
Projected income/Expense total		**−$1886.25**

I&E Worksheet—Year 1

Name _____

Projected monthly income:		$
Projected monthly expenses:		
Mortgage/rent	$	
Phone (office and cell)	$	
Postage	$	
Office supplies	$	
Owner salary	$	
Employee wages	$	
Taxes	$	
Advertising/promotion	$	
Insurance	$	
Legal services	$	
Accounting services	$	
Travel	$	
Online service	$	
Web hosting	$	
Transportation/maintenance	$	
Subscriptions/dues	$	
Loan repayment (startup expenses)	$2	
Miscellaneous (10 percent of total)	$	
Total expenses	**$**	
Projected income/Expense total		$

▲

Sample I&E Statement—Year 2

Wendie Berry Associates

Projected monthly income:		$1,200.00
Projected monthly expenses:		
Mortgage/rent	$0	
Phone (office and cell)	$ 40.00	
Postage	$25.00	
Office supplies	$15.00	
Owner salary	$0	
Employee wages	$0	
Taxes	$0	
Advertising/promotion	$50.00	
Insurance	$25.00	
Legal services	$0	
Accounting services	$ 50.00	
Travel	$400.00	
Online service	$20.00	
Web hosting	$5.00	
Transportation/maintenance	$100.00	
Subscriptions/dues	$40.00	
Loan repayment (startup expenses)	$0	
Miscellaneous (10 percent of total)	$77.00	
Total expenses	**$847.00**	
Projected income/Expense total		**$353.00**

Sample I&E Statement—Year 2, continued

College Bound Consultants

Projected monthly income:		$2,200.00
Projected monthly expenses:		
Mortgage/rent	$ 500.00	
Phone (office and cell)	$170.00	
Postage	$50.00	
Office supplies	$15.00	
Owner salary	$0	
Employee wages	$75.00	
Taxes	$ 6.25	
Advertising/promotion	$100.00	
Insurance	$25.00	
Legal services	$0	
Accounting services	$50.00	
Travel	$400.00	
Online service	$30.00	
Web hosting	$5.00	
Transportation/maintenance	$100.00	
Subscriptions/dues	$40.00	
Loan repayment (startup expenses)	$200.00	
Miscellaneous (10 percent of total)	$177.00	
Total expenses	$1,943.25	
Projected income/Expense total		$256.75

I&E Worksheet—Year 2

Name _____

Projected monthly income:		$
Projected monthly expenses:		
Mortgage/rent	$	
Phone (office and cell)	$	
Postage	$	
Office supplies	$	
Owner salary	$	
Employee wages	$	
Taxes	$	
Advertising/promotion	$	
Insurance	$	
Legal services	$	
Accounting services	$	
Travel	$	
Online service	$	
Web hosting	$	
Transportation/maintenance	$	
Subscriptions/dues	$	
Loan repayment (startup expenses)	$2	
Miscellaneous (10 percent of total)	$	
Total expenses	$	
Projected income/Expense total		$

Earning Your Diploma

Now that you've completed the curriculum necessary to launch your own educational consulting business, you're ready to embark on your new life of college visits and admissions essays. You'll find this foray into home business ownership will be exhilarating, satisfying, and downright fun. After all, you'll be master of your own fate. You can work as much or as little as you wish to meet your financial and personal goals. You'll also never have a boss looking over your shoulder or a daily 5 A.M. wake-up call for a rush-hour drive to the office. And people will actually pay you for doing something you love. What could be better?

Reality Check

At the same time, you need to do a reality check. Under-funding can be a particular problem for college planning consultant businesses, because it's quite common for consultants to earn nothing or even have a net loss in the first couple of years. You'll need to have something to carry you through those first couple of lean years to the profits that are more likely to start showing up in Year 3. In fact, financial experts recommend having enough savings in a readily accessible account to cover six to 12 months of living expenses because you certainly don't want to have to shutter the business before it has a chance to ramp up just because you don't have enough cash on hand to meet your expenses. So before you launch the business, check your personal funding sources, then fill in the gaps with a source of funds like a line of credit or an unsecured personal loan. Then make sure you're frugal with the cash so it lasts.

Naturally, there are other reasons why businesses fail. According to SCORE, the 10 key reasons businesses fail include:

1. Lack of an adequate, viable business plan
2. Insufficient sales to sustain the business
3. Poor marketing plan: unappealing product, poor customer identification, incorrect pricing, and lackluster promotion
4. Inadequate capital, misuse of capital, and poor cost control
5. Poor management skills: lack of delegation, leadership, and/or control
6. Lack of experience and knowledge
7. Lack of managerial focus/commitment
8. Poor customer service
9. Inadequate human resource management
10. Failure to properly use professional advice; i.e., accounting, legal, financial, etc.

> **Beware!**
> Even if you're usually very motivated and disciplined, it can be hard to resist the temptation to slack off when you're homebased. So be sure to dedicate a certain number of hours a day to the business without fail, and remove all distractions, including TVs, best-selling novels, sudoku puzzles, etc., from your office.

It's important to note one last reason why some businesses don't survive: Their owners have trouble dealing with all the freedom mentioned above and instead slack off and neglect to spend as much time as they should on the business. If you have the dedication and commitment necessary to stay focused on your business when the temperature is perfect, the sky is blue, and a boat or the mall is calling your name, then you should be able to make your business work. If not, then you might want to look into taking a time management course or two.

Making the Grade

There are a lot of other proactive things you can do to ensure your own success. To begin with, be sure to establish relationships with business professionals like accountants, attorneys, and computer consultants so you can spend your time doing what you like and know best—namely, educational consulting—and less on the vital but time-consuming, behind-the-scenes work necessary to keep the business running smoothly and efficiently. It's hard to part with the cash when you launch a business, but it really is money well spent.

Take time, too, to learn about the business of managing a business. Chances are you came to this profession because of your interest in and knowledge about education and college admissions—not because you're a brilliant marketer or a savvy financial forecaster.

Often, it's enough to have just a basic knowledge of these areas to keep them under control, and the way to acquire that knowledge is by taking business classes. A community college is the perfect place for that—the classes are affordable, and you should be able to acquire enough working knowledge to make the right decisions in just a semester or two.

> **Bright Idea**
> Be sure to bookmark the IRS' website at www.irs.gov. The agency has a wealth of information available to entrepreneurs, ranging from small-business forms and publications to a desktop calendar tool for small businesses and other pertinent tax information. So while Uncle Sam does take your money, he also gives back value for your buck.

Doing Your Homework

As mentioned in Chapter 7, professional organizations are a good place to acquire information and expertise that can help you be a better business professional and

▲

Beware!

It's easy to give out too much information inadvertently when potential clients call, as Sarah Soule in Burlington, Vermont, discovered. "At the beginning, some people took advantage of me by asking a lot of questions, then didn't hire me," she says. So listen more than you talk, then get their name on the dotted line before you get down to business.

consultant. This industry has several very good organizations, and quite possibly their chief benefit is that they offer access to college tours and networking opportunities. In fact, Mark Sklarow, executive director of IECA, says that at IECA meetings, invariably someone will ask to bounce ideas off the others there. They also bring their promotional and other materials and pass them around to get insight and advice. As a result, any organization gathering will be a great place to listen and learn.

But of course, even with careful planning and good advice upfront, there are bound to be things that crop up after you start your business that you couldn't have foreseen—or simply didn't know about. Even the successful educational consultants interviewed for this book admit there are things they could have done better when they finally made the leap to self-employment. For instance, Charlotte Klaar, the Brunswick, Maryland, consultant, says she should have attended IECA summer training institute when she started her business because "it would have kept me from reinventing the wheel. I spent $12,000 on things that weren't necessary, like hiring marketing people to help me, having forms and contracts developed, and doing other things I could have learned at the institute."

Joan Bress, the Worcester, Massachusetts, consultant, also feels she should have learned more about the business side of running a business before plunging in. "I really didn't appreciate how much work goes into making a business work," she says. "I was very naïve about the whole marketing side of the business, mostly because I had been running a successful therapy practice for 20 years and thought the skills needed would be the same. It took a while to figure out how to do the marketing, and I spent a lot of money on ads that weren't very valuable."

James Heryer, the Kansas City, Missouri, consultant, says he should have been more aggressive early in his career in terms of getting the word out. "It is much like an

Tip...

Smart Tip

Having a detailed and well-thought-out business plan on paper is especially crucial in your first year when revenue is low (or nonexistent). Small-business owners who write down and update their plans annually rarely get into trouble because they've planned for every contingency. So make the drafting of your business plan a priority before you launch your consultancy.

attorney or an accountant starting a private practice," he says. "You have to show potential clients what you can do and how they will benefit from your services. I developed marketing strategies by trial and error, and I should have done it much earlier. It took at least three academic cycles to get everything started."

Judge Mason, the Sedona, Arizona, consultant, and a veteran admissions counselor with 40 years of experience, would have started his business earlier. "I started my business on the side while I was still doing admissions consulting," he says. "I knew I had a gift for reading kids and knowing what they needed. But what I didn't have was an interest in money. So it took me a while to make the transition to self-employment."

Burlington, Vermont, educational consultant Sarah Soule says to watch out for people who want something for nothing. For instance, a family with twins once demanded that she counsel both kids for the price of one. "Of course, I told them since there would be two college tuitions, there would be two fees," she says. Not surprisingly, given the mind-set of the parents, she didn't get the business.

Whitney Laughlin, the New Mexico consultant, concurs that landing those initial clients can be difficult. "As a school counselor, you have a ready-made client base, plus you're coming from a salaried position," she says. "So new consultants are sometimes desperate for clients and make the mistake of pushing kids to schools where they don't belong. But don't use your chips unless you're 99 percent sure the kid is a good match. Otherwise, you're crying wolf and the schools will stop listening to you."

High Achievers

Despite the challenges and the occasional frustrations that come with dealing with people who can be emotional, passionate, competitive, and sometimes irrational about getting their kids into college, the educational consultants interviewed for this book agreed that the rewards are great—both professionally and financially.

On the professional side, the rewards come from helping gifted kids who otherwise might not have a chance to shine. That's why Mason specializes in helping kids who have "gone off the rails because of drugs, alcohol, sex, and rock 'n' roll," as he puts it. In fact, 85 percent of his clients fall into this category, and he credits his willingness to listen to kids and his insight into where to place them for his success.

Joan Bress likes the challenge of working with a range of kids from all walks of life, ranging from those of affluent families who knew from birth which college they would one day attend to first-generation Americans who embrace her suggestions for colleges and like being introduced to new things. "Getting a kid to the right college, then watching as that student grows, develops, and matures, is very gratifying," she says.

▲

Don't Worry, Be Happy

As a new small-business owner facing a potential first-year deficit and a significant learning curve, you may think that advice about being positive and optimistic is ridiculous. But research shows that optimistic people are more successful, better adjusted, and happier all around than their dour neighbors.

So think positive—after all, as an independent educational consultant you're embarking on the opportunity of a lifetime. No more 9-to-5 toiling to improve someone else's bottom line, no matter how worthwhile a goal it may support. No more commutes to the office during rush hour or in inclement weather—you can time your forays into the world to suit your own schedule and avoid the free-way frenzy. And no more bosses looking over your shoulder, noisy co-workers, or annoying daily distractions. You're free at last, and if that's not something to be positive about, nothing is!

Of course, you may find that you'll miss the camaraderie of having coffee with colleagues, strolling the halls of a school and getting friendly nods from kids you've counseled, or having administrative tasks like photocopying and ordering supplies handled for you. But you'll get over that fast because there are simple ways to fill those voids. And did we mention—you're free at last!

So enjoy this wonderful time in your new life. Savor the moment and antici-pate the future with relish. It's a great day when you can do exactly what you want to do and still be able to support yourself and your family while fulfilling your American Dream. Seize the moment, and make it happen. You deserve it.

On the financial side, James Heryer believes that good things come to those who wait—namely, those who pay their dues and work through the learning curve. "One of the reasons I've been successful is my broad background, membership in professional organizations, and certification," he says. "It takes time to achieve these things, but there is the potential to make a lot of money if you do it right."

Achieving a certain income level also means you can afford to do *pro bono* work for deserving kids—something that is very satisfying. For example, Laughlin assists and coaches Native American kids through the nonprofit foundation she founded, College Horizons, which was established specifically for that purpose, while Soule does *pro bono* work for the local boys and girls club. She offers three sessions every fall on topics like college selection and the things a first-generation college student needs to know to make the right choices.

School Daze

No matter whether you decide to specialize or embrace a wide range of opportunities, one thing you will find is that no one day is the same in this business—and on some of those days you'll find yourself shaking your head or otherwise marveling at what comes your way.

Take Heryer, for instance. He once received a call from the office of a highly ranked member of Congress who offered to bestow on him an award of recognition for his success as an entrepreneur. Although he initially thought the call was a joke played by a friend "who is pretty left of center," as he puts it, Heryer eventually was convinced it was legitimate. But he turned down the award and the accolades and publicity that might have followed. "I didn't want to be associated with anything that had a political slant," he explains.

Sometimes the consultant-client relationship just doesn't work out, as Klaar once discovered. She was asked to work with a pair of twins from "the entitled generation," as she puts it. "There was a lot of triangulation going on by the male twin who thought he knew everything," she says. "He didn't meet my deadlines and didn't respond to my calls and emails. Eventually this 17-year-old kid told me to stop bothering him because his family was building a beach house."

That was the last straw. Klaar fired the twins, citing their noncompliance with her contract and offering the emails she had sent repeatedly as proof. Although the young man indignantly shot back that she couldn't walk away from their contract, she stood her ground and told him he needed to be involved or it wouldn't work out. "It was hard giving that money back, but it was important to my sense of ethics to follow through," Klaar says.

Speaking of ethics, encountering situations in which ethics are called into question is an unfortunate side effect of being an educational consultant as kids jockey for position at competitive colleges and sometimes will do whatever it takes—ethical or not—to get in. Klaar learned this firsthand when a parent she was working with whom she also considered a friend dropped the bombshell that she had written her son's college essay. "The kid had a 480 verbal score, and the essay was publishable," she says. "I told the parent, 'This is a great essay. How did he do it?' My friend said, 'You don't think I'd let him write something this important, do you?'"

"I couldn't shade my ethics. I was appalled and asked what message she thought she was sending her children by doing this. I don't have to tell you that I stopped working with the kid, and I'm no longer friends with the mother."

School's Out

It's pretty plain to see that in the final analysis, the main reason why educational consultants enter this line of work is for the satisfaction that comes from helping students achieve their full potential. "I have had students come back to see me five years after they've graduated, and I find that they're really thriving," says Steven Antonoff, the Denver, Colorado, consultant. "I take great satisfaction in seeing that growth, as well as hearing parents say that I've reduced so much of their stress, which in turn created less strife at home. I love being a message of calm in the world of extreme anxiety and hypertension that is college planning."

Now it's your turn to change the world, one student at a time. Good luck, and may you go to the head of the class in everything you do!

Appendix
College Planning
Consultant Resources

Here is a selection of carefully researched resources for you to check into, check out, and harness for your own personal use as you launch your college consulting business.

Please note that these businesses and organizations were all active and viable at the time this book was published, but it's always possible that some of the them may have moved, changed, folded, or expanded since then. We offer this list as a starting point and invite you to do some homework and investigate further.

Attorney Referrals and Information

American Bar Association
www.americanbar.org/aba.html

Attorney Find
www.attorneyfind.com

Lawyers.com
www.lawyers.com

Martindale-Hubbell Law Directory
(800) 526-4902
www.martindale.com

Blogging Platforms

www.Blogger.com

www.Twitter.com

www.Typepad.com

www.WordPress.com

www.WordPress.org

Business Software

Adobe Creative Suite 6
Adobe Systems Inc., www.adobe.com

Broderbund
(800) 395-0277, www.broderbund.com

Dreamweaver CS6
www.adobe.com

Expression Studio 4 Web Professional
Available from Amazon.com, and many computer and office supply stores

Intuit
www.intuit.com

Microsoft Office
    http://office.microsoft.com
    Available from most computer and office supply stores

QuickBooks Pro 2013
    Intuit Inc., (877) 683-3280, www.quickbooks.com

Sage 50 Complete Accounting
    The Sage Group, (866) 996-7243, http://na.sage.com

Certification

American Institute of Certified Educational Planners
    AICEP Commission on Credentialing, www.aicep.org, info@aicep.org

College Consortia

Association of Independent Colleges and Universities of New Jersey
    www.njcolleges.org

College Access Consortium of New York
    http://cacnyinc.org

Consortium of Vermont Colleges
    (800) 776-6675, www.vtcolleges.org, info@vtcolleges.com

Illinois Association for College Admission Counseling
    www.iacac.org

New Hampshire College & University Council
    www.nhcuc.org

Virginia Private Colleges
    (540) 586-0606, www.cicv.org

Computer Support

Geek Squad
    (800) 433-5778, www.geeksquad.com

Demographic Information

American Demographics
www.adage.com

U.S. Census Bureau
www.census.gov

Educational Consultants

Steven R. Antonoff, Ph.D., CEP
Antonoff Associates Inc., (303) 333-8413, http://schoolbuff.com,
steve@schoolbuff.com

Joan Bress
College Resource Associates, (508) 757-8920, www.collegeresourceassociates.com,
joan@collegeresourceassociates.com

James C. Heryer, MA, CEP
College Guidance and Placement, (816) 531-2706, www.jamesheryer.com, james@
jamesheryer.com

Charlotte M. Klaar, Ph.D., CEP
Klaar College Consulting, (301) 834-6888, www.cklaar.com, charlotte@cklaar.com

Whitney Laughlin, Ed.D.
(505) 690-9054, www.whitneylaughlin.com, laughlin@rt66.com

Judge Mason
Judge Mason Educational Consultant, (928) 284-5719, www.judgemason.org,
judge@judgemason.org

Sarah G. Soule
Sarah Soule & Associates, (802) 425-4403

Educational Programs

Academy for College Admission Counseling
www.counseloracademy.org, counseloracademy@comcast.net

California Polytechnic State
University, San Luis Obispo, (805) 756-231, www.calpoly.edu,
admissions@calpoly.edu

Central Michigan University
> (800) 268-4636, www.cmich.edu/global, cmuglobal@cmich.edu

The College Board
> (212) 713-8000, www.collegeboard.org

Iowa State University
> (515) 294-4111, www.iastate.edu, contact@iastate.edu

Marquette University
> Graduate School, Counseling and Educational Psychology, www.marquette.edu

National Association for College
> Admissions Counseling (NACAC), (800) 822-6285, www.nacacnet.org
> info@nacacnet.org

St. Cloud State University
> School of Education, (320) 308-3023, www.stcloudstate.edu, soe@stcloudstate.edu

UCLA Extension
> (310) 825-9971, (818) 784-7006, www.uclaextension.edu

University of Iowa
> Tippie College of Business, (800) 622-4692, (319) 335-1039,
> http://tippie.uiowa.edu, tiiowamba@uiowa.edu

University of Massachusetts Amherst
> Continuing and Professional Education, (413) 545-2414, www.umassulearn.net,
> admissions@contined.umass.edu

University of Wisconsin Oshkosh
> College of Education and Human Services, Student Affairs, and College Counseling
> (920) 424-1475, www.uwosh.edu, geier@uwosh.edu

Wake Forest University
> Department of Counseling, (800) 257-3166, www.wfu.edu

Employee Information

U.S. Department of Labor
> (866) 4-USA-DOL, www.dol.gov

Government Resources

Minority Business Development Agency
  (202) 482-2332, www.mbda.gov

Occupational Outlook Handbook
  www.bls.gov/ooh

SBA
  (800) 827-5722, www.sba.gov, answerdesk@sba.gov

SCORE
  www.score.org, help@score.org

Small Business Development Centers
  (800) 827-5722, www.sba.gov/SBDC, answerdesk@sba.gov

Mobile Credit Card Processing

Intuit GoPayment
  http://gopayment.com

PayPal
  www.paypal.com

USB Swiper
  (224) 677-0283, www.usbswiper.com

Office Equipment (Computers)

Apple Store
  (800) MY-APPLE, http://store.apple.com/us

Dell
  (800) WWW-DELL, www.dell.com

Gateway
  www.gateway.com

HP
  (800) BUY-MYHP, www.hp.com

Toshiba
www.toshibadirect.com

Office Equipment (Phones and Accessories)

Hello Direct
(800) 435-5634, www.HelloDirect.com, xpressit@hellodirect.com

Office Depot
www.officedepot.com

OfficeMax
www.officemax.com

Staples
www.staples.com

Office Space Resource

Office Finder
www.officefinder.com

Office Supplies, Forms, and Stationery

Amsterdam Printing
(800) 203-9917, www.amsterdamprinting.com, customerservice@ amsterdamprinting.com

Office Depot
www.officedepot.com

OfficeMax
www.officemax.com

Paper Direct Internet
(800) 272-7377, www.paperdirect.com

Rapidforms
(800) 257-8354, www.rapidforms.com, service@rapidforms.com

▲

Staples
www.staples.com

Vistaprint
www.vistaprint.com

Online Postage

Pitney Bowes
www.pitneyworks.com

Stamps.com
www.stamps.com

United States Postal Service
www.usps.com

Zazzle
www.zazzle.com

Online Resources

All About College
www.allaboutcollege.com

Campus Tours.com
www.campustours.com

CollegeBound Network
www.collegebound.net

COLLEGE Surfing
www.collegesurfing.com

Common Application
http://app.commonapp.org

Education Connection
www.educationconnection.com

Education Week
www.edweek.org/ew

FAFSA
www.fafsa.ed.gov

fastWEB
www.fastweb.com

FinAid!
www.finaid.org

Inside Higher Ed
www.insidehighered.com

National Education Association
www.nea.org

Private Colleges & Universities
http://www.collegexpress.com/private-colleges

SallieMae.com
www.SallieMae.com

U.S. Department of Education Student Guide
http://studentaid.ed.gov

Pay-Per-Click Advertisers

Google AdWords
http://adwords.google.com

JumpFly
www.jumpfly.com

Postage Calculator

FedEx
www.fedex.com/ratefinder/home

United States Postal Service
http://postcalc.usps.com

UPS
www.ups.com/ctc

Printing Resources

ColorPrintingCentral
(800) 309-3291, www.colorprintingcentral.com

NextDayFlyers
www.nextdayflyers.com

Printing Industry Exchange LLC
(703) 729-2268, www.printindustry.com, info@printindustry.com

PrintingForLess.com
(800) 930-6040, www.printingforless.com, info@printingforless.com

Print Quote USA
(561) 451-2654, www.printquoteusa.com

Promotion Xpress
(888) 310-7769, (510) 357-0238, www.proxprint.com

PsPrint
(800) 511-2009, www.psprint.com

Vistaprint
www.vistaprint.com

Professional Organizations

The College Board
(866) 630-9305, www.collegeboard.com

Higher Education
Consultants Association, www.hecaonline.org

Independent Educational Consultants Association
(703) 591-4850, www.iecaonline.com, info@iecaonline.com

Learning Disabilities Association of America
(412) 341-1515, www.ldaamerica.org

National Association for College Admission Counseling
(800) 822-6285, www.nacacnet.org, info@nacacnet.org

National Association for the Self-Employed
(800) 232-6273, (800) 649-6273, www.nase.org

National Association of Student Financial Aid Administrators
(202) 785-0453, www.nasfaa.org

Publications and Books

ADDitude
www.additudemag.com

College News
www.collegenews.com

Journal of Learning Disabilities
(800) 897-3202, www.proedinc.com

Learning Disabilities Research & Practice
Wiley Online Library, http://onlinelibrary.wiley.com

Next STEP E-mag
Next STEP Publishing Inc., (800) 771-3117, www.nextstepu.com

Start Your Own Consulting Business
Eileen Figure Sandlin, Entrepreneur Press

University Business
www.universitybusiness.com

Scheduling Software

Appointment Quest
(800) 591-9894, (303) 468-7581, www.appointmentquest.com

Cybermatrix
(888) 664-0383, (250) 503-1009, www.cybermatrix.com, sales@cybermatrix.com

ScheduleVIEW
Selent and Associates Inc., (866) 877-8555, (941) 255-3126,
www.scheduleview.com, info@scheduleview.com

Shipping Services

DHL Express
  (800) CALL-DHL, www.dhl-usa.com

FedEx
  www.fedex.com, (800) GO FEDEX

UPS
  (800) PICK-UPS, www.ups.com

USPS
  (800) ASK-USPS, www.usps.gov

Small Business Line of Credit

Chase Business Banking
  www.chase.com

U.S. Bank
  www.usbank.com/small-business

Wells Fargo Business Line
  www.wellsfargo.com

Tax Help and Software

Electronic Federal Tax Payment System
  Department of the Treasury, (800) 555-4477, www.eftps.gov

H&R Block,
  handrblock.com

Internal Revenue Service
  (800) 829-4933, www.irs.gov

TurboTax for Business
  Intuit, www.intuit.com

Web Hosting/Domain Names

Apollo Hosting
  (877) 525-HOST, www.apollohosting.com

AT&T Website Solutions
(888) WEBHOST, www.webhosting.com

Domain.com
(800) 403-3568, www.domain.com

EarthLink
(866) 383-3080, www.earthlink.net

GoDaddy.com
www.godaddy.com

Host Gator
www.hostgator.com

iPage
www.ipage.com

iPower
(888) 511-HOST, www.ipowerweb.com

Yahoo! Small Business
(866) 781-9246, http://smallbusiness.yahoo.com

Glossary

Bluetooth: technology that allows cable-free connectivity between mobile phones, mobile PCs, handheld computers, and other peripherals

Class A office space: leasing term for a building that was built after 1980, has at least five floors and 100,000 square feet or more of space, is situated in a business district, and may have architectural features like floor-to-ceiling windows

Class B office space: leasing term for an older office building that has been renovated and is in a desirable location

Class C office space: leasing term for an older office building in fair condition that has not been renovated and may not be in a very desirable location

Coverdell Education Savings Account (ESA): a savings account established to pay for qualified education expenses. The total annual contributions may not exceed $2,000.

CV: acronym for *curriculum vitae*, which is a written description of work experience, educational background, and skills that is more detailed than a resume; commonly used by people in academic fields

DBA: acronym for "doing business as"; a fictitious business name

Diecut: decorative hole or shape cut into a document (typically a marketing piece)

Double-entry bookkeeping: an accounting method in which transactions are recorded as both a debit and a credit

ESL: acronym for English as a second language

FAFSA: acronym for Free Application for Federal Student Aid, the government form most colleges require students to complete to apply for financial aid

Focus group: a small group selected from a larger population for the purpose of testing and/or evaluating a concept or product

LD: acronym for learning disabled

Lettershop: a company that handles addressing, collating, printing, mailing, list rentals, and other direct-mail services

News release: a one- to two-page article used to promote a positive aspect of the business

Opt-in list: mailing list consisting of people who have given their permission to receive information from third-party businesses

Pitch letter: a persuasive letter written to sell an editor on an idea for a magazine or newspaper article

Primary research: information gathered firsthand from people in response to written or oral questions

SallieMae: the nation's leading source of education funding

SAT: standardized test used by colleges and universities to help select incoming students

Secondary research: information and data gathered by other people

Section 529 plan: a qualified tuition program that's exempt from taxation under Section 529 of the Internal Revenue Code

Single-entry bookkeeping: an accounting method in which transactions are recorded as a single entry

Sole proprietorship: a business with a single owner

Unsecured personal loan: a loan that doesn't require collateral

Viewbook: promotional brochure written by marketing agencies that specialize in university and college admissions; gives just enough general information to induce students to visit a particular campus

Index

Get Entrepreneur Magazine to help grow your business

Don't miss out on must-have tips, techniques, trends and strategies that business owners need to help build and grow their businesses. Learn what other smart business owners know. Subscribe to *Entrepreneur*!

Click on the link below to subscribe to the print edition:

https://w1.buysub.com/servlet/OrdersGateway?cds_mag_code=ENT&cds_page_id=55992&cds_response_key=I1OPBEPDI

or call 1-800-274-6229

Click on the link below to subscribe to the digital edition:

https://store.coverleaf.com/softslate/do/manufacturer/entrepreneur/?utm_source=Coverleaf&utm_medium=Online%2BLink&utm_campaign=PC%2BDigital%2BEdition

Note: Requires a browser to view.

More from Entrepreneur®

EP
Entrepreneur.
Press

Entrepreneur Press is a leading SMB publisher, providing aspiring, emerging and growing entrepreneurs with actionable solutions to every business challenge—ultimately leading you from business idea to business success.

E More titles from Entrepreneur Press
http://www.entrepreneurpress.com/

Entrepreneur.com

Entrepreneur.com is the most widely used website by entrepreneurs and leaders in business worldwide. As the leading small business website, Entrepreneur.com serves its visitors' needs by creating the most satisfying experience with relevant content, logical information management and ease of access.

E Visit Entrepreneur.com
http://www.entrepreneur.com/

Entrepreneur.
NEWSLETTERS

http://newsletters.entrepreneur.com/

Sign Up for the Latest in:

E Online Business	E Sales & Marketing
E Franchise News	E Growing a Business
E Starting a Business	E Hot Off EPress

9 781599 185064